EUROPE MEETS FLORIDA

Encounters with Religion, Psychology, and Culture

DR. MICHAEL J. BAGLINO, ED. D.

Printed in the United States of America

First Printing Edition, 2023

ISBN: 979-8-218-20925-4

TABLE OF CONTENTS

Part IV Politics And History

Part V Psychology And Religion

Dedication

– from the dedication page of my doctoral dissertation at Florida International University – Miami, FL - 1992, I repeat:

"I wish to especially acknowledge the contribution of the faculty and community of Winona State University in Winona, Minnesota. The academic preparation, training, and belief in my abilities are the foundation that made this endeavor possible. Their friendship and Christian service, so characteristic of this university and community, has been the model and standard to which I will always aspire."

And always I did, leading to this third book of a trilogy.

Introduction

This is the final book in a trilogy that began rather recently. My original intent was to serve as a legacy for my children. Let them see a little of what their father experienced and thinks about. Then I decided, why not publish these vignettes, articles, and essays in the form of a book? They won't have to wait until I'm dead. I didn't think I had much time left since I'd been battling some health issues. [see books I and II] I started thinking about this as I began writing for an on-line Catholic magazine, 'Catholic 365'. Having experiences in the areas of sports, entertainment, culture, psychology, history, politics, travel, and Catholicism, combined with a career in education, allowed me to be able to write on such topics. Share and express knowledge; that's what education is.

Winona, Minnesota, is a great little community. [see ch. 5] I lived there for 7 years and received three degrees from Winona State University. Visiting occasionally but not enough. I think of Winona every day. Like many young people, you think you have to leave home and make your mark in the world. Winona did become a home, and my mark has been made. So, let me return to the simplicity of it all. I always used to tell my students that when the s__ it hits the fan, I know where I'm going but would not tell them. Stay away. Well, the fan has been hit in America. What now?

I know this book is entitled *Europe Meets Florida,* and most of it is. Also, it's hit the fan. But the education began in New York and Winona on the way to Europe and then to Florida and back again. So here we go.

Europe Meets Florida: Encounters with Religion, Psychology, and Culture

Part I - Sports and Arts

Chapter 1
Life at a Standstill? Watch a Baseball Game.

Another great baseball game. The score is 0 - 0 in the 15th inning, a 4-hour game. Then just a few days later, 0 - 0 in the 18th inning, a 5-hour game. Houston and Seattle were battling out a 0 - 0 dual shut out. This is but another reason I love baseball - terrific, nothing happening, yet glued to the TV.

Patience, my man, patience; defy any anxieties. When your life is at a standstill, a 5 hr game of baseball will do you good. Focus on the game, focus on God, and keep it there. Author Sally Ferguson indicated how it was life and hope coming to a standstill, all part and partial of our experience with Covid-19 around the world. As she referenced, the ultimate of life at a standstill is expressed in Luke 24 as she expressed it "Good news! Jesus hasn't disappeared; He is here in the midst of upheaval. He walks the road of life with us because He rose from the dead and is now interceding at His Father's side on our behalf!"

Luke 24: 46-48 "He told them, "This is what is written: The Messiah will suffer and rise from the dead on the third day, and repentance for the forgiveness of sins will be preached in his name to all nations, beginning at Jerusalem. You are witnesses of these things."

Just as in baseball, just as in our lives, Men are left on base inning after the inning, and no runs scored. You just can't seem to plow through it all. Well, try it again. What is holding us back? Maybe try a different way, modify your strategies - a bunt, a walk, a stolen base, a pinch hitter. Keep the eyes on the goal and vision of victory while at the same time focusing on the task at hand, each and every inning, each and every batter.

The ultimate standstill in our lives could very well be what my daughter just experienced. Like Jesus being resurrected after three days, her life began after three days of labor. And then, boom. It's all great now, and the pain - no more and forgotten.

Ex 14: 13 "And Moses said unto the people, Fear ye not, stand still, and see the salvation of the LORD, which he will show to you to day: for the Egyptians whom ye have seen today, ye shall see them again no more for ever."

So yes, if baseball or anything in life is at a standstill, focus on God, focus on your goals. Better yet, and more specifically, a strategy is to stand firm and pray and wait on the Lord. Good for Christians and baseball coaches alike.

Psalm 33:20-22 "Our soul waits for the Lord; he is our help and our shield. For our heart is glad in him, because we trust in his holy name. Let your steadfast love, O Lord, be upon us, even as we hope in you."

Exodus 14:14 "The Lord will fight for you; you need only to be still."

Florida is full of baseball, summer, and winter leagues - high school, adult league, college, minor league, and pro. A great place to sit back when life is at a standstill.

Chapter 2
Tenets of Sports Psychology

Never a coach, never really great at the sports I participated in, just above average in some, average in others, as I see it. Loved wrestling and baseball the most, and the two required totally different skills and physical preparations. But I think the mindsets for all sports are similar; that is, focus, commitment, and mental toughness.

Sports are about changing the desired behavior toward the accomplishment of the intended goal. It is self-direction with focus. It is the quest for personal excellence. So, the athlete asks himself what is the area or focus that he wants to improve in and what he must do to achieve it. When an athlete has focus, he has enough concentration to maintain a clear image of the goal or task at hand.

Muhammad Ali, boxer; Roger Clemens, baseball pitcher; Usain Bolt, track star; Dan Gable, college wrestler: they all had the strength of focus. All were champions and examples for all other athletes. Focus involves a number of aspects. By focusing, an athlete helps eliminate any anxiety before his performance, so much so that everything else disappears. He keeps his focus during the game or match and even during practices. And when bad calls or decisions go against him, he can handle it by maintaining his focus. Bolt and Gable were the best at this.

Just because one might have talent in a particular sport does not mean a person would excel. It's practice, practice, practice, and a determination to persevere in that practice with a pledge toward dedication. Along with dedication, the athlete sacrifices other areas of life in order to excel. Areas of sacrifice may include diet, sleep, lifestyle, and avoiding or keeping the right social relationships. Commitment, finally, is to put in the extra time for preparation during the season and for many, many seasons to come. Kobe Bryant, basketball; Don Shula, football; Derek Jeter, baseball; Dan Gable, wrestler: they all had the quality of commitment, and all with a long-term relationship with one team. Admirable.

And finally, champion athletes exhibit mental toughness. It is mental toughness that determines the effectiveness of performance and the likelihood of success. Why is that? It is because mental toughness helps an athlete concentrate on what matters to retain composure and control of himself. There are many aspects to mental toughness. We know an athlete needs physical maturity and development, but mental toughness requires mental maturity and development. This is the result of support, respect, and self-discipline, a form of ego control and proper realistic appraisal. Otherwise, faulty appraisals or perceptions prevent the athlete's correct response to real situations - mistakes. Don Mattingly, manager of the Miami Marlins, took out a pitcher who was pitching a perfect game shutout late in the 8th inning. The next pitcher gave up 3 runs, and the Marlins lost. He followed current managerial patterns of decisions rather than the mental instinct and support of his pitcher. Muhammad Ali did not appraise his physical abilities correctly when in his late 30s; a self-image and confidence limitation and he lost his match against Larry Holmes. For the average snow skier, it is important not to allow the emotional thrill of the ski run to impel you to go down that hill just one more time. That is when you break your leg. Champions work hard, but they know when to limit their work rather than on emotional impulses.

Considering the above, when an individual is involved in sports, he has to self-evaluate and ask himself what his area of focus is. Of course, the ultimate goal is winning the game, but it can change with each practice too. What interferes with his concentration and focus, and how might he improve the situation in each practice? Has he made the decision to commit to regular practice, and prepared to make that commitment for the long term? Finally, it requires an athlete's self-examination in realistically assessing his self-concept, self-image, and mental maturity throughout the process.

In all, it is focus, commitment, and mental toughness that are the integral parts of maturity. It means the ability to perceive the world and oneself realistically and then make the right decisions. The psychology of sport thus requires self-control, self-confidence, ego strength, and realism, all needed for focus, commitment, and mental toughness. This is how you play the game to win.

And what's the bible got to say about all this? Lots. Here are but a few verses. It compares athletes' and Christians' need to train and strive to win the ultimate prize.

1 Corinthians 9:24–27 "Do you not know that in a race all the runners run, but only one gets the prize? Run in such a way as to get the prize. Everyone who competes in the games goes into strict training. They do it to get a crown that will not last; but we do it to get a crown that will last forever. Therefore I do not run like a man running aimlessly; I do not fight like a man beating the air. No, I beat my body and make it my slave so that after I have preached to others, I myself will not be disqualified for the prize."

2 Timothy 2:5 "Similarly, if anyone competes as an athlete, he does not receive the victor's crown unless he competes according to the rules."

Source:

Orlick, Terry. 2007. *In Pursuit of Excellence: How to Win in Sport and Life Through Mental Training*. Human Kinetics Publishers.

Chapter 3
The Christian Nature of College Wrestling

I love watching the NCAA college wrestling championships on ESPN being a former high school and college wrestler myself. And the Olympic wrestling championships, for that matter. The two tournaments are of slightly different freestyle rules but essentially the same. Wrestling was the first Olympic sport going back to 708 BC, and a middle eastern sport for thousands of years. As far as I know, wrestling is the only sport mentioned in the bible. Jacob had wrestled with God, and God spared him and blessed him. His name was then changed to Israel, which means 'struggles with God.' And so, Jacob was forced to confront his failures, fears, weaknesses, his thorns, and his hurts, realizing that through surrender, only God can save him. An exhausting struggle. It was wrestling with God which finally made us know that our lives are not to be easy. Personal growth always involves struggle and pain, but if it is with God, His blessings will follow.

What I also notice while watching Olympic and college wrestling is that so many wrestlers invoke the name of Jesus before and after their matches. Jesus is a part of their daily struggles, not only at match time. They proclaim their debt to Jesus, their Lord and Savior, through it all. These champions, and almost champions, are quite dedicated and, from that, seem to develop confidence, mental toughness, and resilience that never leaves them.

Here is a special note. It has been said that wrestling is the most strenuous sport; its practices and daily disciplines are the most taxing and grueling. I suppose it would have to be if you wrestle with God.

1 Peter 1:13 - "Wherefore gird up the loins of your mind, be sober, and hope to the end for the grace that is to be brought unto you at the revelation of Jesus Christ."

Colossians 1:29 - "That's why I work and struggle so hard, depending on Christ's mighty power that works within me."

The amateur wrestler is called to always be mindful, sober, and alert. Such are the fruits of dedication and commitment. With that and the daily struggles of practice and prayer, victory follows.

Psalm 62:6 - He only is my rock and my salvation: He is my defence; I shall not be moved.

Further, I have never met a wrestler of champion quality who was not mentally tough. Mental toughness is that psychological edge that allows an individual to triumph over his/her foes. Mental toughness includes clarity and focus, allowing the competitor to manage the stress and pressure confronting him/her. Mental toughness is the mindset of a winner in that they will execute excellently and consistently. With ongoing preparation, they develop a belief in themselves that is solid and unwavering. Mentally tough.

Philippians 4:13 "I can do all things through him who strengthens me."

Proverbs 3:26 "For the LORD will be your confidence and will keep your foot from being caught."

And confidence, a belief in themselves, and a belief in God. Through endurance of those grueling practices, through repetition, through the drilling and sweat, through the prayer, comes the confidence of that execution and victory. They fight through it all to stand firm at the end and love it all.

James 1:12 "Blessed is the one who perseveres under trial because, having stood the test, that person will receive the crown of life that the Lord has promised to those who love him.

James 1:4 "Let perseverance finish its work so that you may be mature and complete, not lacking anything."

Seems we are in a wrestling match with God all our lives. But as adults well past the age of the wrestling of our youth, it is not struggling and wrestling against an opponent on the mat. Rather, we struggle and wrestle now against powers, against principalities, against all sorts of spiritual wickedness - within us and without us. We move from struggle to struggle; we prepare, we self-discipline, and we pray to engage the foe with God's word.

Chapter 4
Celebrity Impersonators

Found myself in the celebrity impersonator industry for about 15 of my 20 years, singing professionally. It began in 2003 when as a local Sinatra tribute artist, I decided to go to an impersonator convention in Las Vegas and join in with all the others. How much fun it was, and it was a thrill to meet them all as if they were the real deal. I never lost the thrill over the years. The problem is: so many lose their identity, act like the character 24/7, and can be really obnoxious. So many of the Sinatra impersonators I met thought they were tough guys, acted rude, and were very competitive. Grow up!

Another problem was explained to us by a fellow impersonator participant upon exiting McCarren Airport in Vegas. "Just wait," he said. "Soon, this will turn into a gay industry, performing transvestites and cross-dressers." A few years later, I found myself on a nationally televised ABC-TV celebrity impersonator show taped in Orlando called 'The Next Best Thing.' The contestant judges assured me I did a very good bit singing 'The Best is Yet to Come.' "You're a good singer but not sounding so much like the man himself, Sinatra," commented one of the comedian judges. "True," I retorted. "It was your sound system." They freaked. Actually, I agreed with them and did it for the humor. No disrespect was given from both side of the stage, but I did lose to a Cher transvestite impersonator. I wondered if our Vegas friend was on to something.

We met so many impersonators of great talent, I might add. From Michael Jackson to Tina Turner; from President Bush to President Obama; from Marilyn Monroe to Mae West; from Danny Devito to Sammy Davis, Jr., I could go on and on like James Bond, John Wayne, and Bruce Willis. You name the celebrity; we met him or her. My favorite became my best buddy, Luciano Correa. He was Dean Martin and totally devoted to him all his life until the day he died; that's Luciano, who died as Dino was long gone. We formed a 'Rat Pack' and traveled the country performing.

There can be some racial incidents too. After our 5-10 minute bit each in the showcase, I was approached by a young lady during our group photo shoot. She knew so much about a conversation I had earlier in the evening and acted as if she knew me. How did she know me? This white woman was none other than Tina Turner on stage in full body make-up, and we did have a conversion when in costume. Similarly, after one of our Rat Pack shows, I was having a drink with my Sammy Davis, Jr. buddy. He is Italian and Puerto Rican, not black. I was pointing to him for an audience member who met us in a local bar. He could not understand why he did not see him, though he was sitting a few bar stools from me. "Oh," I said. "That's him, the white guy over there. He had make-up on stage."

Another of my Sammy Davis, Jr. members was a real MF in the vernacular. Arrogant, snooty, hot stuff. He just would not help us break down after the show. It apparently was too below him. I fired him on the spot. He ran off after we almost had a physical confrontation, and I haven't seen him since. There are plenty of Sammy Davis, Jr. impersonators. All trouble, I might add.

Every September in Orlando, Florida is a gathering of celebrity impersonators and tribute artists from around Florida and around the world. Called the 'Sunburst Convention,' performers will arrive from far-off places like Canada, California, London, and Germany. We meet to perform and catch the eye of agents willing to represent us. The impersonators take on the very look and sound of the celebrity. Often times you're not sure if he's the real thing, especially in public. Tribute artists may not look like nor sound exactly like the performer, but they honor the celebrity's work of whatever artistry - music, dance, acting, or politics. President Bush was great; the Bette Midler terrific; a phenomenal Elvis or two.

At our last visit in 2016, we paid special homage to the slain gay victims of Pulse Night Club in Orlando. I suppose. Led by

Dame Edna and Jackie Gleason [one in the same person], it was a very touching and special evening of honor and respect. But to us, it seemed that this is what The Sunburst Convention had become, extreme liberal politics and anti-Christian comments. Mae West ran away from me in a huff when I said a good word or two about President Bush. I recalled the conversation with our friend at McCarran Airport in Las Vegas in 2003. Yes, perhaps he was on to something.

Part II Culture and Education

Chapter 5
Winona, MN - Island City of Nature

Let me add beauty to that title. And so, I could write about this island city on the Mississippi River in southern Minnesota, filled with both beauty and nature. As the Mississippi River widens, at some points as much as 5 miles, it is an island settled and developed for some 200 years originally as a lumber town. It is an island surrounded on both sides by forest filled 600 ft. bluffs. To the east of the river is Wisconsin, and to the west is Minnesota. Winona is that small island city in between where good fishing abounds, where there is water skiing in the summer and snow skiing in the winter. Where there is ice skating in the winter and hiking and bike riding in the summer through its myriad of nature trails and lakes, it is a city overlooked by cliffs and the scenic Garvin Heights, where legendary Princess Wenonah fell to her death. Where it is surrounded by rich farm land, and both pumpkins and apples grow abundantly. A culture of cheese and wine tasting along its winding roads north and south of the river. It is the home of St. Mary's University and Winona State University, listed by 'U. S. A. Today' as the safest college campuses in the midwest. A lovely city to both live in and go to college.

But no, I'm not going to write about that. Rather, I am going to discuss another aspect of its nature: foxes, flies, bats, and the dreaded mayflies - its loveable pests.

Pete L. was a biology major at Winona State College [now university]. He loved animals and even seemed to have a way of communicating with them. Near St. Mary's University is a fox farm, and I believe that is where Pete acquired his pet fox, unless he caught it himself, probably. So we, his college roommates, had to live not with a pet collie or lab but with a fox. He came home each day, let him roam the yard, fed him, etc. I know they eat rats, mice, and insects, but I do not know what he fed them. He fed his pet fox but not for long. Eventually, he just tied him up with rope in one of our clothes closets. Then he started to forget to feed him. It probably went a week of reaching into the closet in the morning for our clothes before going to class until the inevitable happened. Yes, the closet started to reek, and the growls got a little louder each time any one of us would reach in there. I wonder if our class mates ever noticed the stench in our clothes. One momentous morning I reached in there once again for a shirt, pair of pants, and shoes. I noticed the rope that held him was bitten clearly; thus, he was a-loose in there. OMG! Uh oh! I know he's angry. His growls get louder and louder. I stepped back a step. The fox stepped back. I stepped back again; he stepped back. I slowly stepped back yet again, and he did the same still. Still growling, it was clear he didn't want me there. I reached for a shirt, and he showed himself, teeth and all. Boom! And another Boom! I slammed that door as fast as I could, and simultaneously, every item and box from two levels of shelves pounced on top of that fox. Phew! - I escaped some serious trouble just in time. That fox was trapped and buried, and it wasn't for another week that Pete finally got around to freeing the fox. The next animal dilemma to deal with was the chickens our landlord secretly raised in the basement. The rooster woke us each morning. But that's another story.

Bill G. was also a biology major at Winona State. He ended up teaching jr. high school biology for many years afterward, but not until he wreaked havoc on some of his best buddies. Genetics, one of his favorite classes, allowed him to do his own experimentation. House fly heredity, and larvae were under study. There were dozens of test tubes available full of the larvae. Not quite winter, he thought, why not secretly drop a few of these available larvae in his buddy's winter boots at their 60 W? Howard Street apartment. He wasn't using them yet, so this would go unnoticed as he continued thinking to himself. And his theory of house fly production proved correct. Each day more and more house flies appeared from apparently nowhere until probably hundreds were living there with those good buddies of his. Swat a fly here, swat a fly there. It went on for weeks. Where are these pests coming from? We pondered. Open the windows and shoo them out, or spray them as a last resort. Keep them out of our food at dinner time. It took many weeks before they were finally all gone after we found those stashed away winter shoes. It's funny when you're young that you can put up with all this crap and still have a smile on your face. We never knew it was Bill G.'s doings until months later.

Bats are everywhere in Winona. Miserable and ugly-looking things. Walking at night, you can see them flying around and hanging from trees. I threw a shoe at a bat hanging from a local elm one night. Boom! Got it! I hit him on its head, and that's all it took to kill it. If you live on the top floor of an apartment, good luck. They just love to crawl in under your door at night. They love to live in your attic too. One summer as a visiting professor at St. Mary's University, I had the unfortunate pleasure of being given one of the empty summer dorm rooms as my residence. Don't you know they would try to squeeze under the door and invade your domicile? And that was the bottom floor! I had to plug up the doors with towels each night to prevent such from happening. It worked. But in the early 1960s, bats were especially menacing to women. These were the years of bouffant hairdos, and Minnesota girls just loved that style. The trouble is bats also love to plant themselves within those coiffures of hair. Restaurants were vulnerable. For some reason, bats got into these downtown establishments and chased everybody away, especially the women. They'd leave their meals and bills and never return, all screaming on the way out. Not to worry, really, as they only eat insects, not people's necks. Further, since the mosquito is the Minnesota bird and extremely plentiful in the summer, bats are actually a desired resident as mosquitos are its favorite food and can consume as many as 1,000 insects per hour.

Not to be outdone with the above menaces of nature are the Mississippi River's most populous pest, the mayfly. Born beneath the Mississippi River, they emerge, and these disgusting little creatures fly all over downtown Winona by the millions. So many that snow plows are needed to scrape away all those dead in the streets and on the sidewalks. Landing on anything white is preferred, and they live for only a day. But a day is enough. Bats love them, even in the daytime. One unsuspecting casual summer Winona day, not attuned to the news that week, I decided to visit downtown on a bicycle. It hadn't occurred to me that this was the week of the mayflies. As I approached Charlie's Bar and Cafe, my favorite hangout, millions, I say millions, were swarming all over downtown. You had to cover yourself, your face, your eyes, your clothes, like a swarm of locusts you'd see in that famous movie 'The Good Earth.' And they stick, especially to walls and cars. Sticky and tough to get off even after they die. Did I mention disgusting?

Here are four pests of the natural habitat of Winona. It is not all beauty, and there's more: leeches in the river, mice, rats, snakes, and poison plants amid its abundant forests. I'd still live there in a heartbeat, America's best-kept secret - Winona, Minnesota.

Chapter 6
Literary Author Mario Puzo and the Italian American Experience

Of Mario Puzo, Time Magazine said, "If Mario Puzo never writes another word, he will already have earned the title of 'Godfather of the Paperbacks.'" Well, Puzo's The Godfather and 'an offer he can't refuse' has surely become part of our language. This may place him in a niche of American letters. And he has certainly assured a place in American numbers. The enormous popularity of The Godfather, which has sold more than 14 million copies, has made Mario Puzo one of the most sought-after novelists and screenwriters.

Critics have generally suggested that Puzo's works are useful to literary scholars due to the sociological and historical content of his themes—the themes of Italian immigrant struggle within the context of the American urban environment and industrial change. Yet, organizations such as the Italian American Foundation and Italian Anti-Defamation League have pointed out the negative influence of his writings on the image of Italian Americans. For example, 85% of all mob movies have been produced since the 1972 Godfather movie. They maintain that equating Italians with mobsters and buffoons has been the downside of his literary success. Thus, his legacy remains controversial. On a personal note, I recall when, as a lead actor in one of my theater performances in Minneapolis, a newspaper writer asked me how I acquired my gangster demeanor and style. "What do you mean?" I replied. "I am not acting like a gangster; I'm acting like my uncles from Brooklyn, who themselves were far from being gangsters." In other words, she thought that just because you acted in a NY Italian manner, you were a gangster. LOL. I suppose if you speak with a southern twang, it conjures up all sorts of images of provincialism and racism. And it does for so many people today. I'm not so sure it was Puzo himself who helped create a negative image of Italians.

Mario Puzo was born to immigrant parents, Antonio and Maria Puzo, in New York City's Hell's Kitchen in 1920. He and his four brothers and two sisters were raised by their mother in this predominantly Italian neighborhood. Recognizing the social intricacies and organizational nature of this community, Puzo learned about the unique relationships among Italians that mainstream American culture prefers to refer to as the 'Mafia.' To Puzo, this was not a network of criminal behavior but just the way society worked. Yet, until the day he died, Puzo maintained that he had never met a so-called gangster, and all his books were based on research and composites of characters he had met or observed throughout his life, similar to the above.

That life's experience spanned quickly from an inner-city New York neighborhood to a civilian public relations administrator for the United States Air Force in Europe. While in Europe, he met his wife, Erika Lina Broske, and had five children. It was while in Germany that he was encouraged to write about the many characters and stories he would tell his friends and fellow employees, which he had learned about while growing up in his New York neighborhood. As we always said, New York is full of characters, and Mario certainly met his fair share. Growing up consisted of spending time at the local kids' hangout, the Hudson Guild Settlement House. There, he was the captain of the settlement house football team and the president of his gang. Quite a title he gave himself. More importantly, as a background for career success, he often visited the library of the Hudson Guild, where he read stories and even the complete works of Dostoevsky. His youth was not quite finished. WWII found Puzo, and he was drafted and stationed in Germany. He returned to the United States to work as a civil service administrator. During the late 1940s and 1950s, he studied literature and writing at Columbia University and the New School for Social Research. He began writing short stories and completed his first novel, Dark Arena, in 1955. Set in post-war Europe, it is today considered a minor classic. This was the first of a series of works combining sociological insights with a historical context. Its literary force was the focus on the dehumanizing effects of war for both the conquerors and the conquered.

Shortly after the publication of Dark Arena, Puzo had a severe gallbladder attack on Christmas Eve. After taking a cab to the V.A. Hospital, he fell into the street. Thoughts of dying, yet finally being a published writer, led to a personal decision towards wealth and fame. The Godfather and subsequent Godfather Papers were intended to make money, and their enormous success was beyond his wildest dreams.

In 1965, Puzo wrote The Fortunate Pilgrim, his second novel. Semi-autobiographical, this novel depicts a second-generation Italian immigrant matriarch dedicated to her six children. It was considered a talented merging of social history combined with sensitivity to the nature of relations between individuals. Gay Talese congratulated Puzo for creating "perhaps the best novel ever written about Italian immigrants in America."

In the 1960s, Puzo deliberately intended to write best-selling novels. The greatest of his efforts, The Godfather, and the trilogy, as depicted in the motion picture sequels, detail the rise and fall of a mafia don, Don Vito Corleone, and his sons Sonny and Michael. Sociologists recognize its depiction of a family's frustration in realizing the American dream. That is when avenues toward success are blocked. People will seek alternative and even illegal, means of achievement. Other less serious critics noted both the novel and films as well-written, suspenseful, and dramatic by an extremely talented storyteller. Especially noted are his realism and believability of the social setting and characters. But then, others criticized Puzo for portraying such characters in too favorable a light. John G. Cawelti wrote, "The Corleone family is presented to us in a morally sympathetic light, as basically good and decent people who have had to turn to crime in order to survive and prosper in a corrupt and unjust society." Puzo responded in Publisher's Weekly, "I was awfully surprised when people loved The Godfather so much. I thought I had shown him as a murderer, a thief, a villain, a man who threw babies in the oven... so I was astounded when I was attacked for glorifying the mafia. It's a little tricky. I think it is a novelist's job not to be a moralist but to make you care about the people in the book." Yet, he was also quoted saying, "I'm sort of proud they're so clever in crime. In fact, I even believe they have a natural gift for it - the southern Italians and Sicilians - it was the only way they could stay alive." It is reminiscent of the southern Italian and especially Neapolitan character trait of 'arrangiarsi,' making do in the struggle for social survival.

The phenomenal success of The Godfather led to the selling of film rights and subsequent screenplays, underworld-based novels, and made-for-TV movies. Earthquake [1974] was one of a series of extremely successful disaster movies and Puzo's third screenplay. Its enormous success led to screenplays for Superman I and Superman II. Subsequent novels include Fools Die, based on the gambling scene in Las Vegas; The Sicilian, a semi-fictional historical and revolutionary tale set in northern Sicily; The Fourth K, a political thriller roughly based on a distant Kennedy cousin; and The Last Don, depicting a crime family's struggle and disintegration amidst a modern backdrop. The Last Don was made into two TV movies. His final novel, The Family, was released in 2001, posthumously. Mario Puzo died from heart failure in Long Island in 1999.

As for his own success, Puzo humbly related that he was just another Italian success story, perhaps not as great as DiMaggio or Sinatra, but his own experience would serve us well.

Sources:

Baglino, Michael. 1999. *Mario Puzo in Italian Americans of the 20th Century*. George Carpetto, Editor. Memphis: Wimmer Cook Books.

Puzo, Mario. 1972. *The Godfather Papers and Other Confessions*. New York: Putnam.

Chapter 7
Critical Race Theory and the Marxist Putsch

We hear of what Dr. Thomas Sergiovanni, Ph.D., used to warn America about back in the early 1970s: the coming dictatorship of the curriculum specialists. Well, it's here now, and the battle is heating up between these curriculum dictators and American parents. Gender ideology and Critical Race Theory (CRT) are two major current curriculum impositions in our public schools. Right off the top, I'll say let us get our children out of the public schools and into private Christian and Catholic schools to save this country.

Now, Critical Race Theory (CRT) is an academic approach that insists on the connections between race, racism, and power in America. It is a Marxist social construct that challenges the very foundation of the American order and our constitution. According to these neo-Marxists (communists), everything is founded upon race. They argue that since race is the most significant part of American lives, there are unequal outcomes in our society, both legally and economically. This ultimate inequity is the result of this unjust society and must be transformed. One important note: the word "communist" is never used by liberals and progressives since it has always had a negative connotation in America and is repelling to most. Therefore, although it is never used, it is exactly what Marxism is - an authoritarian, atheistic ideology toward political, economic, and social control.

Transformation of our society would then come through the systematic attack on American institutions, its culture, and its heroes. Antonio Gramsci is probably the most influential European social and economic theorist of the 20th century. Gramsci is one of the intellectual godfathers of the Black Lives Matter (BLM) movement's leaders. He is referred to as a neo-Marxist for proclaiming his opposition to capitalism and supporting public ownership of wealth and property. Since capitalist societies are controlled by ideology and cultural means, Gramsci called for a systematic attack on its ideology and the breakdown of its culture. This includes an attack on Christianity, which Gramsci believed to be the glue of the culture. Only through this could the people's consciousness be altered, paving the way toward the progressive civil society they envision.

Similarly, Herbert Marcuse is a German atheist philosopher with profound influence on BLM and the Critical Race Theory (CRT) mindset. Marcuse maintained that both continents, Europe and especially the United States, were actually repressive societies - politically, economically, humanistically, and sexually - and called for freedom-seeking youth to rebel against them. This included criticism of the foundation of their culture, Christianity.

He called for the disaffected and alienated to unite en masse against the prevailing structure. The movement is ignited by funding from activist groups and curriculum efforts supported by individuals like George Soros, other leftist billionaires, leftist organizations, and tax-funded governments.

How does the change evolve? It happens through college admission policies with race-based criteria, through curriculum guidelines in public schools, by reinterpreting and rewriting the history we were originally taught, supporting anti-racism activism like BLM, funding such programs through corporate and government sources, defunding the police and replacing them with mental health officers, and through propaganda efforts in attacking so-called racists, including Christians.

Lots of problems with all of this, especially for those of a Christian background. It seems that Frederick Douglass and Martin Luther King, Jr. both based their civil rights efforts on the Christian vision of the human person as expressed in the U.S. Constitution. CRT also opposes the U.S. Constitution. It opposes nuclear families of a mother and father, supports gay rights and marriage, legalized abortion, legalized drugs, and prostitution.

CRT calls itself anti-racist, yet it advocates for cruelty and discrimination against white people. They say present discrimination is necessary to end past discrimination. I mean, who would believe in convoluted illogic and irrationalism? The alienated, the misinformed, and the anti-Christian forces of the centuries, that's who. Marxism has moved on from its assertion of an oppressed working class to oppressed minorities of non-white races. It claims success does not come from Christian values; it comes from white privilege.

And so, identity politics becomes of major importance. These Marxist academics will then give support to Black Lives Matter [BLM], which attempts to force awareness of this inequity through propaganda and urban turmoil. They aim to bring racism into the consciousness of the American people and then force change from their guilt. They give support to CRT to promote change through our youth. It's better to say that they force their social experimentation upon our nation and its youth. And it is an experimentation, as Marxism has never worked in human history. 'Thy Kingdom Come' takes time, not through violent revolution.

Source:

"Fighting Critical Theory." October, 2021.
 CatholicVote.Org.

Chapter 8
Adolescent Development in America

Another one of my favorite lectures, whether it be in psychology, sociology, or education classes, is Erik Erikson's theories of lifespan development. Let me give you a glimpse as we focus on adolescence and ask you to think about your own solutions to some case dilemmas - just like in class. I chose this stage, adolescence because I believe this stage presents the quintessential problem in America: our relationship with teenagers, who are an alienated group for sure.

Essentially, Erikson believed that an individual is faced with eight crises in life, from infancy to late adulthood. Throughout the various life stages, the child will transition to another stage, facing the crisis successfully or somewhat successfully. The functioning of the adult or late adult in society is dependent on the previous stages. If fortunate, the child, now an adult, can catch up if any needs are not fully met. If not so fortunate, the adult must bear some heavy burdens. For the adolescent, the crisis revolves around identity. A teenager's identity is achieved when they can answer the question, "Who am I?"

They have developed inner uniformity and completeness through the roles and value systems with which they identify. To the adolescent, gender, ethnicity, race, and the role models by which they are influenced have a great effect on identity. They need to belong. Self-esteem and self-concept are raging issues. For example, to this author, heterosexuality, Catholicism, Italian heritage, professional occupations, athletics, and athletes are what he identifies with. His friends are the same, except for the fact that they grew up in a Jewish neighborhood, which also had an influence. His self-esteem came mostly from participating in sports, and it carried over into adulthood.

Cognitively, adolescents go through significant changes as they physically grow. They begin to think more abstractly and develop reasoning skills. Therefore, the curriculum is designed to meet these changes with courses in algebra, history, and literature.

Richie M. was a senior in high school and pretty much an alcoholic. He came from a well-to-do professional family, and when it came to academics, he performed well below what was expected of him. He even shows up to class after the lunch break somewhat intoxicated and can be nasty. Algebra is the class in particular where he acts up. Yet, he is one of the school's better athletes, and teachers have failed to contact his parents about his behavior. His teachers are on the young side and are fearful of confronting him.

Kenny G. is 17 and in 10th grade. Most 10th graders are 15. Kenny flunked 6th grade, and because his family has moved around often, he has missed out on yet another year of school. They are not a poor family but certainly do not match up to the upper-middle-class, college-bound population of this school. His clothes are not the same, lacking the modern style designer dress of what might be called a bougie group of students. He smokes and drinks a bit. He is not athletic, but he certainly has the potential for it. He's a street tough but does not associate with his classmates. His family has never visited nor supported him in school, and they themselves never graduated high school. One day he decided to pick a fight with the school's top athlete, BMOC, and he got whooped. It embarrassed him before all the others.

Theresa S. was one of the few Afro-American students in a predominantly white private high school located in an upscale community. Just about all the students arrived at school each morning in their Mercedes or BMWs. She was driven to school by her parents, and one day, because of a scheduling mix-up, she was forced to take the city bus home that evening. She was beside herself. She couldn't be seen doing such a thing and refused. "Take the bus?! They'll laugh at me!" she said. Talented in sports and academics, she did not perform quite as expected, so her parents decided to transfer her to a public school.

There she excelled.

And so we ask, discuss, and/or write out:

What's the problem or problems?

What should the teachers have done?

What should the school administrators have done?

What should they have said to each of these students?

What should they have said to the parents?

What would be the best way to approach the future for each?

And my community college students, just a year or two beyond adolescence, have great insight.

Sources:

Adams, Frank D. 2001. *Case Studies in Educational Psychology*. RoutledgeFalmer.

Berk, Laura. 2018. *Exploring Lifespan Development*. Pearson.

Chapter 9
What are People Like Today?

Matthew 25:35 ”For I was hungry and you gave me food, I was thirsty and you gave me drink, I was a stranger and you welcomed me.”

1997: We befriended a family, a mother and four children in Gainesville, FL. The children were fun, and one particular relationship was with their oldest son. I became somewhat of a mentor, and we would venture out to the University of Florida's Ben Hill Griffin Stadium and run up and down the stands to get in shape. Empty during the week, we had the entire stadium to ourselves. We actually started a trend there. It is now a common practice at the stadium. The four children were good students, impressive, and smart-talking. Their mother, Ms. Diana C., had done right by them. In fact, she always tried to do the best for them. However, small problems arose. Shortly after the children's visits to our home, small items and cash started to disappear. We overlooked it and, in spite of it all, were glad we got to be friends.

After a year there, with little opportunity for employment in Gainesville, we decided to move to the Twin Cities, Minneapolis, and St. Paul, where I used to live. One day before leaving, I described to Ms. C. what it was like there and the Minnesota culture of social justice concerns. Besides the cold and snow,

Minnesota shows much concern for the poor, the disenfranchised, and the alienated. Dorothy Day Residence Shelter for the Homeless is one such institution that exemplifies its action, not just lip service. Food banks, free medical clinics, homeless shelters, and donation programs of all kinds are common in the area.

We left in September. On December 24, 1997, Christmas Eve, we received a phone call. "Michael, it's Diana. We have arrived with our furniture. Can you help us unload our moving van into a storage facility? We were given a month's voucher in a local hotel from 'Mary's Place,' and Catholic Charities until the shelter has a place for us." Sarah and I were shocked. As she explained later, she researched the opportunities for families in her situation in the Twin Cities on the internet and followed us up here. These things just do not exist in Central Florida - no jobs, not much welfare to speak of. She planned it all out. How? I do not know.

During the 2,000-mile trip, she shared driving responsibilities with her associate friend while her four children sat in the towed car. I don't think that is legal; I'm not sure. So, Ms. C. detached her car from the truck, we unloaded everything, and then she took off with her children and associate. He then disappeared, never to be seen again.

What a nice Best Western hotel Catholic Charities put her family up in, along with additional food vouchers. After a month, they moved into a very small apartment at the homeless shelter. With comfortable accommodations, they settled in. One morning, a reporter from the Minneapolis Tribune ventured into the Mary's Place facilities. By chance, she ran into Ms. C and her four children. Let me remind you that they are very impressive, good-looking, intelligent, and well-spoken, without the often-times Afro-American dialect. The reporter was drawn to them and decided to interview them, and she wrote an article that was published in the Tribune. Suddenly, there it was on the front page one Sunday.

"Wow, look at this! A three-page article full of photos of Diana and her kids," I exclaimed to my wife, Sarah. What an impressive article detailing her background, her personal struggles, her ordeal in coming to Minneapolis, and her children. "How terrific," I thought. Mary's place soon found them an apartment in Section 8 housing in a Minneapolis suburb. No sooner had they moved in than their apartment was filled with gifts from all throughout the state of Minnesota. The citizenry of Minnesota was taken aback by her story of struggle. They felt so much sympathy and compassion that from Winona to Rochester, Moorhead to Bimidji, St. Paul to Mankato, International Falls to Duluth, their new home now had furniture, TVs, food, toys, clothing, and gifts of all kinds. And they continued to receive gifts for over a year. "Oh! I should've mentioned I needed a car in that interview," she shouted as more gifts arrived one day.

Except for the gifts, Ms. C. planned it all. The truth is, she kept every bit of it. The graciousness of Minnesotans is granted. They were hoodwinked and bamboozled. Gracious yet naïve, they were purposely taken advantage of. No, she connived. She even partook in TV interviews on behalf of homeless families at the Dorothy Day Shelter. Probably two or three years later, she now owned a home in North Minneapolis. How was that?! Mrs. C. knew how to milk the system. She hadn't worked a day ever since I met her, as intelligent as she is. Minnesota is now populated by many domestic immigrants from Chicago, doing the same—copycats. Minnesota is now populated by many illegal immigrants doing the same. One of the highest-taxed states in the union, Minnesota was way ahead of the federal government with all its social welfare programs. President Biden's administration is fulfilling that same agenda nationwide with the illegals. People aren't stupid. If it is there, take it. Taking it is easy, along with a naive populace that encourages it. Welfare, of course, exists to help families and individuals emerge from their dire conditions in life. But the same old lesson returns; it breeds a culture of non-productivity and leeching. Those who want to take rather than contribute.

As for Ms. C's children, they are grown now and have families of their own. I guess she did well for her children again. I don't know about the subsequent domestic and illegal immigrants. I don't know them personally. We still keep in touch with the older son and daughter, with phone calls but mostly on Facebook. Their children are all school-aged, ready to face the world. Minnesota, especially Minneapolis, is not the same as before the 1990s. Riots and extreme ideological propaganda have helped deteriorate this once relatively crime-free and Christian culture. May God be with them.

Related Source:

See ch. 10 in this book,

or Baglino, Michael J. "Homelessness and Naivete." www. Catholic 365.com

Chapter 10
Homelessness and Naivete from both Sides of the Corridor

1 Corinthians 14:20 "Brothers and sisters, stop thinking like children. In regard to evil be infants, but in your thinking be adults."

We didn't know. I mean, we trusted all our priests, Christian missions, and social justice efforts. This is not an uncommon attitude. We have sympathy for the homeless, compassion, and give out a few bucks here and there to the street beggars.

Being tired of the Miami rat race, we found ourselves in Gainesville, FL, for about a year. Certainly, it's a nice town, not too large, with a university atmosphere and a rural culture in and about. I taught some education classes as an adjunct at a local campus of a Catholic university. My wife was a homemaker. There was a blurb in the Gainesville Sun. Our church, which we had just joined, was having a small reception in honor of the recently successful fundraiser on behalf of the local homeless population, and all were invited. "Oh, how nice," we said to ourselves, and we decided to attend. We really wanted to be a part of our Catholic community and get to know more people. We certainly were active participants at our Miami church, St. Rose of Lima, and felt we could contribute again in some way.

Patting themselves on the back, I suppose; that's what these small events are, or even big events, to help raise some more money. We drove to the dining hall at our Holy Faith Catholic Church. There was a clear sign directing visitors to the entrance. We were casually dressed, wearing jeans, T-shirts, and sneakers. We arrived at the door and peeked in. A little surprised, we saw men in suits and women in gowns all sipping champagne. Fancy. Well, perhaps a little uncomfortable, we thought we should enter anyway. A priest came to the door. I suppose to greet and welcome us. How nice.

"Yes?" he said to us. "Can I help you?"

"Uh, well, we are here for the church event," we replied.

He took a good look at us. We didn't have on a suit and tie or gown. Rather, as I said, jeans, T-shirts, sneakers, and a beard belied my college professor identity. Did I mention one of us was black? Always a concern. We were just regular folks, as I thought of us.

"Oh, you need to go around back with the rest. There are refreshments and appetizers there," said the priest.

Well, what do you think? And who do you think was in the back and not in the dining area of the church? The other homeless, like us, he apparently surmised. We were shocked. He told us to go to the back with the other homeless. The priest hesitated, and then as we left, he realized the obvious boo-boo of judging us from our looks and became a little embarrassed. It was supposedly open to all, but he still did not invite us in. Yes, we left. I've got nothing against the homeless, but we were insulted. I hope you can understand. You know what I call these people at the reception? Liberals, not Christians.

Proverbs 14:15 - "The simple believeth every word: but the prudent man looketh well to his going."

So, I see it as trusting people without realizing that priests and other donors for the poor could be prejudiced too. Well, that was our first lesson.

Proverbs 22:3 "The prudent see danger and take refuge, but the simple keep going and pay the penalty."

I always considered Minnesotans a naïve lot. I know we are naïve, but not nearly as much as them. Of course, they do know about business, whereas we don't. Some of the best and nicest individuals I have ever met are from Minnesota. Nice, but naive. They are definitely people that look out for others, personally and socially, and have social justice concerns. I met a fellow in St. Paul, MN, who told me this story about his recent visit to Miami. There's lots of crime in Miami, mind you. He was with friends and family, walking under the Interstate 95 overpass. You don't do that there. They came across some homeless people sleeping in cardboard boxes.

"How could they ignore these people like this?" they said to themselves. In Minnesota, they house all their homeless.

"Hi, we're visiting from Minnesota. Can we help you out with anything? We'll come back with some food for you."

So off they went to find a local restaurant and came back with some Chinese food—chow mein, egg rolls, wonton—plastic silverware and plates, the works. The small group, their disheveled, dirty selves, were still there waiting. Sure enough, they looked at the food and out came their own knives. They roughed them all up badly—parents, children, friends. They cut their clothes, not themselves, thank God, and scared them all to death. They took all their money and credit cards and, oh yes, took the food. It was easy for them. Don't you think they should have known better?

Chapter 11
Is There Such a Thing as Black English?

Before we can answer that question, we need to know what we mean by the terms Standard English, Creole, and Patois. Standard English, we might say, is the norm, the way we ought to speak and write. We see standard English in the newspapers, in popular magazines, and in books. We hear standard English on radio and television spoken by news broadcasters, on regular talk shows, and on weekly series programs. We write standard English because we learned the correct form in our schools, public and private. In sum, it is the language spoken, heard, and written by the majority of the culture. Though the English of the UK, Australia, and Canada are similar to the American style, there is variance to a certain degree. So, these mentioned nations and cultures have a slightly varied concept as to what standard English is in their own countries. Accents vary, expressions, words, and spellings may vary, but there is enough in common to call these our common language and even consider their form part of a standard worldwide English. Because of the changing globalization process of current history, such variations of English are now referred to as World English.

The word Creole refers to a person of European descent mixed with a person of African origin. This person resides in the

Caribbean or Latin America. He learns English; he knows an original African tongue. Consequently, as the new culture grows, the language spoken is modified from the original. In the case of local creoles [being from South Florida, I'm speaking of the Caribbean region], the local culture's speaking patterns evolve into a creole. This is a mix of the original language of Africa and the language of the colonialist. Thus, those inhabiting Jamaica begin creating and speaking a new language, British English and the African dialect of it. Linguists call it a creole or patois. Those living in Haiti began creating and speaking a new language called Haitian Creole, French, and the original African dialect. Those living along the Caribbean rim may mix the original African with Spanish. The PBS-TV documentary series, 'The Story of English,' illustrated that language is constantly in motion. Always changing and developing, language progresses by bubbling up from below the experiences of the people speaking the language. New words are developed, and new expressions and ways of expressing. In fact, English itself was once a creole language. Spoken in northern and eastern Europe, its people made their way to the northern islands now known as the UK. As it became a language of the majority, eventually accepted and normalized by all, its standardization was set in stone. The standard English of the UK then spread through the world through exploration and colonization, only to mix with the language of the local population. New creoles were formed.

And so, linguists view creoles and patois as a non-standard form of English, a new language nonetheless, as it transposes grammatical forms as well as vocabulary and accent into a new form. Here are some examples from Jamaica:

I will be right back = Me soon come.

What's up? = Wah gwann? Whappen? Whe yu a seh

Over there. - Ova deh.

Don't mess with me. = Nuh romp wid mi.

Everything is good. = Mi deh ya. Evryting criss.

And what about Ebonics, the current term used for Black English? This can be best understood as we explore its origins. In this case, let's look at Daufuskie Island in the Hilton Head, South Carolina area. Here live descendants of the first slave Africans brought to work the original plantations of the south. The first slaves of this island spoke Gullah. This language is a mixture of western African languages and southern standard English. They still speak it to this day. The bible has been translated into Gullah for the local population. A dictionary of Gullah has been created. It goes something like this:

"De fus Wuk house bin buil' yah 'roung sebbinteen sixty-nine." Or - The first work house was built here around 1769.

"De ol' jail buil' yah een eighteen od tow bin fuh white prisonnus." Or - the old jail has been here since 1802 for white prisoners.

In addition, subject-verb construction has been transposed so that speakers maintain the order of the original African language.

I bin der yah. = I have already been there.

I bin had dat befo. = I already had that before.

Thus, verbs in African dialects may often times put the verb before the subject or the adjective after the noun, then translated accordingly. And it stuck; a new language was being created.

This is but a scant presentation of a complex assessment of Black English. There is a history, an on going cultural development, not only of Afro-American culture and language but every culture around the world that comes in contact with English. So what am I saying? I am saying we have English creoles and patois developing everywhere in the world when a culture confronts the need to know and speak English. That need is usually for business purposes. However, whether it be Southeast Asia, Latin America, or Africa when the local language meets English, their own input twists and modifies the language, the ongoing task is to teach standard English worldwide - a world English, and yet be open to the newer versions as they grow.

Black English is one of these newer versions. For example, there are about 17 African nations that use creole English as their national language. Nigeria, Sierra Leone, and Liberia are but a few. The English Creole dialect of eastern Sierra Leone is a dialect that parallels Gullah spoken in South Carolina and Georgia. That is Black English too. This is the language they have created. This is the future. 'Yes' is the answer to the above question.

Source:

Baglino, Michael J. 2022. "English as the International Language." *You Only Live Thrice*. PenguinWriters.

The Story of English. 1986. PBS Mini Series.

Chapter 12
Culture and Loneliness in America

Psalm 27:10 "Even if my father and my mother have forsaken me, the Lord will take me in."

Philippians 4:19 "My God will supply every your need in accord with his glorious riches in Christ Jesus."

We are foreigners in our own country and even more so with this abrupt social revolution underway. It is almost as if we are strangers in a strange land. The problem, says Archbishop Charles Caput [2017], is that our children and grandchildren are not foreigners. They seem to fit right in, at least trying to, and at least for now.

Loneliness, in this regard, has been around for many a millennium. It is that state of being that we recognize every so often that actually is a fact of our human existence. It seems to be buried within us but may bring with it melancholy or even depression. Simultaneously it carries an anxiety that begs us to seek a solution to this deep angst. We are free to do so, and so perhaps finding some meaning in our lives will help us remove the discomfort. I say meaning, not drugs, not escape, not rebelliousness. What is our responsibility? Can God do anything about it? How can a more purposeful and engaging life remedy it all?

This, to me, is the crux of it all - our existential reality and God. It makes me hungry and thirsty. Hungry for meaning and thirsty for Jesus. This culture of ours begs us to seek Him; it is an alienating culture.

Ours is a capitalistic culture, probably the most capitalistic-oriented culture in the world. To this author, nothing intrinsically wrong with that. Everything is in moderation. Yes, corporate America has its faults, its abuses, and anything detrimental that large-scale organizations can impose upon a culture. This is the subject of another chapter or book. Here let us recognize the cultural influence on our personalities and behaviors because of it. Our capitalist-oriented culture is very individualistic and with it, the concept of personal autonomy. It is up to us. We gradually recognize our own uniqueness, talents, and individual strengths, hopefully in a healthy way.

The downside is that it increases our loneliness or at least helps us to recognize our aloneness. We are separated from society, and we become anxiety prone. The world overwhelms us, and it is threatening. Submit to the authority of this culture and the administrative state that eventually comes with it, or escape. Conform or become estranged. Lose your individualism or integrity, or find alternative routes. Therefore, capitalism brought with it the freedom to create and become the version of ourselves we choose. But at the same time, powerlessness and anxiety. Along comes religion to save the day, but which one? Even Catholicism falls short [the religion of your humble author], at least in this lifetime. The cross of Christ can be difficult to bear.

We end up psychologically thinking it all out. I call it murmuring. We philosophize, intellectualize, imagine, and develop ambitions, all to ease this angst. We experience, take risks, and create. It is the logic of our soul that calls us to reach out to God in the midst of it all. We can't rest until he answers with what we are looking for - truth, goodness, and beauty.

We look at the same time to get our minds off ourselves to contribute and be productive for others. What can I do for the body of Christ, for society? "Ask not what your country can do for you. Ask what you can do for your country." It certainly is not collecting government-guaranteed incomes. Productivity and contribution are the only cure for our angst.

Want to talk about alienated and a stranger in a strange land? Father Walter Ciszek, S. J. was a Polish American priest from Pennsylvania. [Baglino, 2022] He is part of a beatification and canonization process of the Roman Catholic Church, the road to sainthood. Beatification is the Catholic Church's recognition of a dead person's entrance int heaven. Canonization is whereby the church declares that a person who has died was a saint, and hopefully, you can read his story and recognize that for yourselves. Detailed accounts of his story can be found in his books, *With God in Russia* and *He Leadeth Me.* Upon entering the priesthood, Father Ciszek was sent to Albertyn, Poland, in 1937. He then volunteered as a needed worker in the then-Soviet Union to be available as a priest to the Russian people. Big mistake in this author's eyes. To make a long story short, he was arrested and sent to the gulags in Siberia.

For 23 years, he bore the suffering of solitary confinement, torture, violent interrogations, and 16-hour workdays in -20 to -40 below zero temperatures, all with being denied food and clothing necessary for such an ordeal. He was forced to survive among criminals, thieves, and murderers while a political prisoner. Released from prison but forced to remain in Siberia, Father Ciszek worked as an auto mechanic but was watched relentlessly so as not to practice his religion as a pastor to local Catholics. What meaning did he find in the years 1937 to 1963 while imprisoned and hounded by the KGB? He decided that if he were to spend these years as a prisoner and auto mechanic, he would devote his all and abandon himself to the almighty. Accordingly, if Russian found this the way to improve their country, then he would do his part and contribute to Soviet society as best as he could along with the blessings and graces of God. Along with Jesus, he would work in the mines and work in the auto garage, all while doing his utmost. He received many Soviet honors and medals for his work. To Father Ciszek, his survival was a matter of divine providence. He returned to America in 1963 through the political intervention of President Kennedy, a prisoner exchange. Existential reality and God. We don't have it that bad.

Source:

Severson, Randolph. *A Catholic Soul Psychology.* Benson, North Carolina: Goldenstone Press, 2013.

Baglino, Michael J. "The Canonization of Father Walter Cizsek." *You Only Live Thrice.* Kearney, NE: Morris Publishing, 2022.

Part III Europe and Florida

Chapter 13
Athens, Napoli, and Joe Matone: What I Learned by Living in Europe

In 1967 I headed off to Seville, Spain [Sevilla, Espana, as we expats say]. My father accepted a position as a Civilian Personnel Officer at the nearby Moron United States Air Force Base. Off he went with my mother and sister into a home outside of Seville. I arrived that summer. My father followed his stints in Athens, Greece; Zweibrucken, Germany; and visited all parts of Europe during his stay. He even took a post in Vietnam in 1975, just before it fell to the Vietcong. Never got there myself.

But as for our European experience, it certainly had a profound effect on all of us. We actually melted into all of it. My father left, being tired of the New York rat race and even tired of the American culture itself. Being raised Italian family from Napoli, he always believed himself to have a strong Greek genealogy. This all turned out to be true, more European than American plus Greek roots. Point of interest, ancestry.com indicated to me that I was southern Italian, yes, but also 20% Arabic due to my mother's Sicilian side.

Let's move on. Language, of course, is the first cultural significance of Europe. It motivated me to learn some Spanish, renewed my childhood Italian, and refreshed my high school and college French. Never got that proficient, but enough to get by. So many Europeans know so many languages being the countries in close proximity to each other. Uneducated taxi drivers or waiters will get around with 5 or 6 languages under their belt. Later in life, I began to realize the cognitive benefits of language, especially in old age. I do believe people who speak more than one language have an extra added layer of intelligence inserted within them. Parlez-vous french fries?

We had a car, but really it wasn't necessary. It is easy to get around by bus or train, and governmental subsidies made it all very inexpensive. Rome and Paris had their subways too. Traffic is horrible, and gas is so expensive that I really didn't mind public transportation. It becomes a way of life. To me, Paris has the best subways or metros, as they call them. So frequent and so on time.

Speaking of Paris, the cafe lifestyle is addictive. Same as in any of the major cities and even smaller towns and villages. A real pleasure stopping along the way, having a coffee or pastry, watching the comings and goings, and witnessing an argument or two. Europeans express themselves vociferously but keep their distance. In America, a raised voice is a fight. Experienced it many times. Walking the city is the way - Rome, Paris, Heidelberg, London, etc. so much to see and so pleasant an experience. I always had to warn European tourists in Miami not to venture too far as they may run into danger.

The international perspective dominates. National chauvinism is frowned upon, and the message is intercultural communication. It led me to a doctorate focusing on international development education. The problem was when I recently spoke to a Polish visitor here in South Florida. He just could not understand the Trump mentality. He really didn't understand the American mentality. "He doesn't think like a European." I would tell him, but it just didn't sink in. It had to be his way. I am not arguing here, but the European proximity to every place else in the world, plus their unique history, certainly influences their perspective on matters. Super capitalism and living oceans away from the world affect American thinking. Think about it.

Of course, with internationalism its major current, politics is everything for Europeans. Everyone talks about politics in Europe, and they are so passionate about it. Learned to be passionate about politics while in college, and having worked for the Department of Defense myself, we were very attuned to what the American mission was; that is, economic development and protection of Europe against the USSR. Beginning with the Marshall plan after WWII, the trend toward government and corporate collaboration was instrumental in what was referred to as 'the economic miracle'. Europe began to boom, and its turn from almost third-world status to one of the world's highest standards of livings blossomed in a relatively short period of time. What d'ya think? While working on my doctorate, I researched a paper on the 40th year of NATO. It's role has been forever changing from a small group of 12 to over 20 and today, even perhaps extending into Ukraine. While sitting on a hill overlooking the Mediterranean in Mykonos one afternoon, a large U. S. NATO battleship floated by, and most remarkable and extraordinary it was. It sunk in what we were doing there.

Government plays a very big role in every European country. Yes, a bureaucratic state in each and every nation there. It brings them good health care, good schools, good public transportation, and high taxes, but the interior of their homes is falling apart. Can't get local government permission to do anything, and it takes so long to get that permission if you do get it. So many transactions are done under the table. Someone pointed out to me once the famous shoe industry of Europe and Italy especially. Who wouldn't want to walk around in some beautiful Bruno Magli shoes? They are all exported out of Napoli, famous for their shoes. But, looked up in the yellow pages, you won't find one shoe factory listed. The government apparently turns a blind eye.

I love the art scene in Europe. Galleries and museums are everywhere and all topnotch. You find the finest art even in its subways, elevators, train stations, and bus depots. While visiting the Prado in Madrid, I could not leave. My history professor once told me of the time he hid inside Le Louvre at night after all doors were locked. I guess you could do this in the 1950s. When in Perugia, I took a people mover into the center of the small mountain on which the central town of Perugia was perched. From the center, you take an escalator that brings you up to the central piazza of Perugia at the top of the mountain. But throughout that short journey were amazing historical art works of many centuries back, along the people mover and up the escalator, all lit with just as artistic lighting. Art is everywhere.

Its architecture is art and history. And I believe it is psychologically healthy. You know when you wake up in the morning that you are part of history. You are rooted and anchored in a culture. Here in South Florida, everything goes after five years. They call the 1960s central part of Naples, Florida, its historic district. With that is the warmth of the people, making it easy to meet others. People like to talk in Europe, find out what you think, especially if you know the language. Expats are interesting to talk with. They have many stories from their many experiences and want to make friends.

And family life still dominates in Europe. Though Europeans may have drifted away from the church, the family culture still seems to be in tact. God wants it that way, and at least they have held on to this. Children are not so much the center of life, and parents are more authoritarian, maybe except in Italy. Generations of the family will still live together in the same home, and there is a healthy connection between the generations. Extremes of alienation are avoided or at least attempted to avoid. The continent is not perfect, of course, save for Switzerland.

Finally, I learned about the food. Organic, fresh, tasty, and fiber-rich. Spain, Italy, and Greece, to me, have the best. Restaurants abound, and commonplace foods here are so expensive in the states. I buy an artichoke in Publix for $3.50 but just a single Euro in Paris. And living is not as expensive as you may be led to believe. Well, there are so many examples of differences, pluses, and minuses. For Americans, Europe being a western civilization culture, life is livable for us. There are still daily siestas in southern Europe, and they approach life with more of a relaxed sense. When sitting at a restaurant table, that table is yours until you leave. You won't be rushed out. If, for some reason, they need the table, you are greeted with a small glass of brandy, gratis. It means time for someone else but in a nice way.

To me, I'd rather live in Europe if I could. Wouldn't you? The lifestyle, culture, and demeanor of the people are more fitting; however, I do think health care is better here, no matter what some might say. Especially my HMO and specialist care in this part of Florida. And, if living there, I wouldn't have any baseball to watch. Pluses and minuses.

Chapter 14
5 Special Florida Restaurants We Frequently Visit

These memorable restaurants stand out for us in Florida. There may be better restaurants around but none better than Il Bellagio or Columbia. Elisabetta's and Eggscetera are surely up there, while Roland Martin Marina Tiki Bar is listed only for our own experience. Any visitor, I think, would still enjoy it there. It is not a bougie Palm Beach County spot, for sure.

IL Bellagio, W. Palm Beach, has always been a regular visit for this family. My cousin [also named Michael Baglino] was executive chef for many years. Located at tourist mecca City Place, across from Trump Tower, is an Italian Piazza smack in front of spectacular water fountains. Listed as the number 1 Italian restaurant in the Palm Beaches by Tripadvisor, it is a gathering place for all in Palm Beach County, and the atmosphere is addictive. Never have we had a meal there and stayed less than 3 hours. The staff won't push you out, as in many American restaurants. People strolling, music playing, you just can't leave. Its menu includes a variety of home made recipes just like grandma made. But of course, my cousin learned his recipes from our grandmother, Autelia Baglino. The artichokes, the sausage and peppers, linguini frutti di mare, and agnolotti are all straight from Napoli via Greenpoint, Brooklyn. And many other dishes.

Elisabetta's is an upscale trendy spot located on Flagler Avenue in downtown West Palm Beach just across from the Palm Beach Yacht Club. A little pricy but really a warm and fun atmosphere. Maybe a little noisy at times. Their location in Delray Beach definitely is noisy if you want to know. The location is a plus as you can walk nearby downtown after dinner. They might rush you a bit might. It is crowded. Sitting at the bar for late afternoon specials when not that crowded is a treat. Everything is handmade, and the decorative ambiance contributes to a positive experience. Seems to be for yuppies and professionals of the Palm Beach set. If you see anything negative when googling Tripadvisor, it is probably from seniors. They're a very critical lot.

Eggscetera is another Palm Beach County restaurant we frequent. As the name indicates, it is a breakfast joint and closes at 3 p.m. Breakfast restaurants are very popular in South Florida, and I guess they cater to the senior crowd. A family-owned restaurant, the service is impeccable, and nobody dislikes Eggscetera. Every dish, from pancakes to waffles, to omelets, to fruit dishes, and any combination thereof, is to die for. There have been many restaurants at this location that could not make it. Palm Beachers are very picky. But Eggscetera has been here for over ten years.

Columbia is not a Palm Beach restaurant, but it should be. Our favorite is the Columbia in Ybor City, Tampa. Cuban and Spanish dishes are its specialty and authentic as they can be. You are definitely transported in time and place. Listed by Tripadvisor as the number one restaurant in all of Florida, it does have other locations since its initial successful establishment in 1905 in Ybor City. Those in Sarasota and St. Augustine are terrific too. With old-world charm, you can't be disappointed here. The flamenco dancers thrill, and other than the standby paella and arroz con pollo, you will love the ropa vieja, eggplant riojana, or any of the salmon dishes. Columbia is yet another place claiming the best key lime pie in Florida. Ybor City's Columbia is a great experience.

Honestly, I would say the **Roland Martin Marina Tiki Bar** does not have the best food. We list it only because we often visit on the way to Ave Maria, Florida. Located in Clewiston, this tiki bar sure lets you know it is country and you are out of Palm Beach County. It is an hour and 15-minute drive from central Palm Beach County through miles and miles of sugar fields and the infamous Belle Glade. Country music, Lake Okeechobee, and the fishing culture reign. Fishermen come in for a bite. You can catch an airboat ride, dock your boat, and fish your heart out. So what do they serve besides chicken wings, fish sandwiches, fries, and Okie hamburgers? None other than the gator, gator tacos, and catfish. Don't know how good. Never tried them.

So that's it. Let it be known Palm Beach County has an Italian restaurant on every corner, along with a Pubix and Walgreens. From 1 star to 5 stars, they are all good. Breakfast joints are popping up all over the place. Cuban and Latin establishments are also everywhere. I could have listed a few, like Don Ramon or El Sabor, Cuban and Venezuelan. What else do seniors do but go to restaurants and tell themselves how multicultural they are?

Chapter 15
Spain, Morocco, and Marijuana

Young people can be real stupid. Mea culpa. In 1967 at the age of 23, I took my first trip to Europe - Spain. My parents and sister lived there in Seville, not far from Moron Air Base. A Civilian Personnel officer for the Dept. of Defense, my father had decided to take this position and move there, being fed up with New York and America in general. He should be living here now, right?

So, off I went on a TWA 747 with two bags of marijuana in the front pockets of my jeans. Told you young people can be real stupid. Not only that, I mailed them back to APO through the military post office to my P. O. Box address in Winona, Minnesota. You can do that in those days. Still stupid. When I saw the movie 'Midnight Express about a young, naive American college kid caught with marijuana in Turkey and his horrible ordeal, I cringed. It could have been me. I thought God was protecting me; He wanted me to be writing these books later in life.

I went to Morocco, just a short trip from Algeciras, a city near Gibraltar. College students went there to cop some hashish in Marrakesh. I didn't; I just wanted to see Morocco. I met a gentleman in the street who looked like a businessman. He recognized me as a young Spanish fellow and was very surprised to find I was American. He spoke English, Spanish, Arabic, and who knows what else. So many people in this part of the world speak many languages. After a short conversation and realizing I was an American graduate school student, he figured I was probably about all the other naive Americans looking for some drugs. He then pointed out to me the fellows sitting in the streets up against the buildings. They were disheveled, dirty, hands shaking, and obviously destitute. "See that?" he said. "Hashish! Losers!" He continued, " Drugs have been in this part of the world for thousands of years. You Americans have just discovered it. It is no good for you and only for losers." I got the message.

I did stop with the recreational drugs shortly after that as an attribution to growing up, especially after starting to teach in the Minneapolis schools. Have had mixed feelings about drugs ever since. Well, it is for youngsters, I'd say to myself. Let them experiment and have fun. No longer do I believe that. Drugs are no good, period. It is unChristian. Oh, I joke about it. Will feign a hit for a laugh once in awhile. I'm no square is the message. But really, drugs are no good.

Galatians 5:21 "Envy, drunkenness, orgies, and things like these. I warn you, as I warned you before, that those who do such things will not inherit the kingdom of God."

1 Peter 5:8 "Be sober-minded; be watchful. Your adversary the devil prowls around like a roaring lion, seeking someone to devour."

My understanding is that marijuana and hashish are a lot stronger today than yesteryear. And with it comes more incidences of related drug use, poor academic and job performance, and cognitive deficits. Plus, excessive use can lead to hereditary defects, immune system defects, loosening of inhibitions, and anti-social behaviors. All scientifically proven. Strong doses and prolonged use can lead to psychosis. I know an 80-year-old lifelong marijuana user whose doctors keep telling him to stop using it as they claim it is the cause of his addiction, psychosis, and need for prescriptions. "Nonsense," he says. "I'm OK; I've been using marijuana all my life." Case closed.

Are our bodies and minds our own to abuse as we please? Can we face our future without intoxication? Are there other ways than drugs to help develop our character and human potential? Dr. Gregory Bottaro, in his book "The Mindful Catholic," calls all to grow in personal awareness and self-discipline through three actions: being sober, alert, and mindful. He calls it mindfulness, the need to spend each and every day being aware of the present moment and accepting it. Mindfulness is a practical approach to trusting God so as to feel the safety and security God intends for us.

I look at it this way. You pray the Lord's Prayer, and you will be as high as you could ever be. Marijuana only distorts thinking. God intends for us to be mindful by taking responsibility for ourselves. By being mindful, we master our emotions rather than being mastered by them. By being mindful, we live by faith rather than by fear and anxiety. Mindfulness also allows us to be more decisive in our lives, standing for our convictions. Finally, when mindful, we become individuals who look for growth challenges and become better versions of ourselves. I call this maturity and character development. Drugs have nothing to do with maturity and character development; it is adolescent.

1 Corinthians 3:16-17 "Do you not know that you are God's temple and that God's Spirit dwells in you? If anyone destroys God's temple, God will destroy him. For God's temple is holy, and you are that temple."

1 Peter 5:7 "Cast all your anxieties on him, because he cares for you."

Not marijuana.

Sources:

Bottaro, Gregory. 2018. *The Mindful Catholic.* Beacon Publishing

Heerma, Wik. 2013. "What's Wrong with Marijuana?"
The   Philadelphia Trumpet.

Chapter 16
3 Europeans Visit 3 Special Communities in Central Florida

A French Insurance executive, a member of the German Bundestag and a Belgian M. D. all decided to visit the Lake Okeechobee area one weekend some 35 years ago. They were visiting the United States for the first time and enrolled in a Professional English training program at Florida International University. I had the honor of presenting the program to them and during that process they had become acquainted with each other. Each had also identified themselves as Christians. Rather excited about finally visiting the U. S., they were impressed with the campus and No. Miami Beach area. The beaches were beautiful, the restaurants excellent, nightlife abundant, and the standard of living rather high. Look at the map of Florida, they exclaimed in the middle of a conversation. There is a giant lake in the middle of the state. Wow, this must be a wonderful area - less crowded, more rural, bustling with Florida nature, full of alligators, not cars. Let's go there during our time off. I remained quiet.

Mind you, Florida of the late 20th century and today to me is essentially of suburb of New York City. It is Long Island, NY transposed into Florida, the Long Island of the 1950s. This particular area of Miami was and still is a trendy place. You'd better wear designer clothes, drive a Mercedes or BMW, and golf your head off whenever you feel. These three gentlemen saw all they envisioned about the country they finally got to visit and loved it.

Packed and ready to go on Friday afternoon, they returned Monday morning for classes – mouths dropped ! How could this be? This is the United States? Never saw poverty like this in my life ! - mentioned the German. Nothing beautiful about it ! - said the Frenchman. This is nothing of what is presented to us when we hear of the United States ! - exclaimed the Belgian. The word squalor was used often.   Yes, I responded. It is an area totally ignored by the rest of us in So FL. I thought it could be an educational trip for you, so I said nothing.

Pahokee, Belle Glade, and Immokolee had the one time distinction of being labeled the poorest communities in the United States.   Home to predominantly migrant farm workers from Mexico, Jamaica, and Haiti, these communities struggle to barely survive. Yet, they are only 40 miles from the richest community in America, the island of Palm Beach, FL.; a straight shot down Southern Blvd. from the Atlantic Ocean. The major portion of its residents live in trailers and shacks in the interior of town and along the miles and miles of sugar fields.

Worlds apart from the rather upscale communities of the nearby Palm Beaches, St. Mary's Catholic Church is home to a historic 16th Century Russian Icon known as 'Our Lady of Bethlehem.' Previously owned by the 1st Czar of Russia and the Romanov family, this Icon of Jesus and Mary was prayed before many a Russian peasant for nearly 500 years. After the 1917 Communist Revolution it was mysteriously transported to the United States and landed in the possession of the Edward Kahn family of Palm Beach, FL. A story in itself. Upon his death, this wealthy Jewish philanthropist decided to donate the Icon to St. Mary's Church along with $2 million, saying that the Icon must be in the hands of the poor to serve the poor.

Pahokee was a one time agrigultural community of Irish settlers from the north. It is home to country singing star Mel Tillis. Today the newly constructed church of St. Mary's serves Pahokee's poor migrant farm worker families with the 'Our Lady of Bethlehem' Icon prominantly displayed. It is a sight to behold in America's poorest town.

St. Philip Benizi Catholic Church also had a distinction. It is located in the town of Belle Glade, once labeled as the AIDS capital of America. It is also located directly across the street from the one time community hospital where so many AIDS patients resided. So overwhelmed by this catastrophe, upon the subsiding of this epidemic, Palm Beach county decided to close the hospital in Belle Glade and rebuild approximately 2 miles to the north. The majority of the Haitian and Afro American community it serves are migrant farm workers who also survive through the generous contributions of St. Vincent de Paul and other Catholic charities such as the Knights of Columbus throughout South Florida.

An acquaintance and former heavy weight professional boxer, once had the unfortunate experience of having a flat tire while driving through one evening. Five toughs approached him, beat him up and robbed him of all his money. Actually not far from the church. Don't drive in Belle Glade at night.

Our Lady of Guadelupe Parish in Immokolee is located another 40 miles west. Clearly it is the largest church in the area, again predominantly poor migrant farm workers. All masses are in Spanish or Haitian Creole. When you visit, you know you are not in the United States but rather a transplanted rural community from the central areas of Mexico. Its prime characteristic, not so much a parish of immigrants but rather of an elaborate social services system of Catholic Charities offering the basic needs of food, shelter, clothing, household items, stability and education and they deliver. To say this is an impoverished community is not an exaggeration.

A resident confided in me some of the unfortunate the activities forced upon the local police department. Once after a murderous altercation, the local government had the responsibility of returning the deceased [an illegal] back to Mexico. Occasionally the locals get into a little clamor after some beers at the cantina or home parties in their dilapidated trailers. Tempers flare, punches thrown, gunshots fired. People die. Mostly illegals with little information about them, the city has the responsibility to take care of the deceased. This is Immokalee! With no funds in the city government and with no information coming forth about them from the local population, how are they to return the body to Mexico? Who is he, where to in Mexico, and who has the money to do so? So, occasionally the local gator population will have to take care of it. Yes, that's right, they dump the body deep into the Everglades - problem solved.

For sure, these communities and churches are worlds apart and with a different mission from the neighboring rat race and modernistic, traffic dominated cities of Miami, Naples, Fort Lauderdale and W. Palm Beach. Bougie the young people say. You might want to get away and visit for a weekend but don't forget to bring your fishing pole, bring your gun, maybe bring your bourbon and six pack. Definitely your rosary. But I wouldn't tent out and sleeping bag it. Swarms of grasshoppers and sundry other insects during the summer months not withstanding, with perhaps an occasional bear, panther and /or boa or two. Yes, the Catholic Church and their communities struggle in Central Florida.

Adapted from:

Baglino, Michael J. 2022. "Three Catholic Churches and Their Communities in the Everglades." *Catholic365.com.*

Chapter 17
A Pilgrimage to Ave Maria, FL

Ever go on a pilgrimage to a special place of God's calling? Let me introduce you to our special place - Ave Maria, in the diocese of Venice, Florida, in Southwest Collier County.

To get there from W. Palm Bch. It is about a 2 1/4 hour drive and a 1/2 hour drive from Naples. Passing Belle Glade and La Belle, you will arrive at the edge of the Everglades, with new urban development in spite of the location.

"Fire, Fire!!!" Shouted the state attendant on the way south of Belle Glade. Brush fires in the swampy glades? Winter drought. We were forced to turn around and come another day. The times they a-changin'. The Everglades ain't what it used to be. Upon our return some weeks later, we entered Immokolee, a migrant farm worker community. It is probably the poorest town in Florida and clearly of a dominant Mexican culture. At the far end of the town, proceeding toward Ave Maria and Naples is but another Seminole Casino. This is Miccosukee community land, one of the tribes of the Seminole Nation. The Casino thrives; Immokalee does not.

Ave Maria is a master-planned community located east of Naples at the edge of the Everglades. Founded in 2005 by Thomas Monaghan, original owner and CEO of Domino's Pizza, the spiraling Ave Maria Catholic Church is the town's main focus, located within its central Annunciation Circle. It is their reason to be and stands like a landmark on the horizon, as stated by one of its main architects, Harry Warren. It is also home to Ave Maria University and Law School. Highly regarded academically, maintaining a Catholic identity is one of its main missions as a university. Around Annunciation Circle are a variety of businesses - hair salon, sports bar and cafe, and Italian and Mexican restaurants. Sarcastically I can say that residents and visitors can take in some Mexican food without visiting nearby Immokalee. But that isn't so. There is a growing interchange, and I would encourage any visitors to do the same.

Further around the circle, there is also an insurance company, real estate offices, bookstores, clothing stores, and a nearby Publix to boot. It earned "The Community of the Year Award' for seven straight years. Most of the homes and residences were and are constructed by Lennar, Pulte, and Del Webb. Adjacent to the university, strolling and bike paths throughout this community is a common past time. Comfortable living, for sure.

From the Ave Maria Parish website, the distinctive characteristic of the church is its interior steel structure. The outside 30 ft. sculpture of the Annunciation depicts Archangel

Gabriel's announcement to the Blessed Virgin Mary. At the altar are icons of the 12 apostles positioned beneath the Cross of Christ. All are a sight to see as well as an engaging and spiritual place of worship in which to pray. Of course, it is a very vibrant Catholic community of parishioners.

Guided tours are available, and again from the parish website is a picture/quote from Saint Padre Pio, "Let us become saints so that after having been together on earth, we will be together forever in heaven." Visiting Ave Maria will help you on that path. It is a little bit of heaven itself. I can say that any visit here is a refresher and restarting point toward your own personal sainthood.

Source:

Baglino, Michael J. 2022 "Three Everglades Towns Florida Ignores." *Catholic365.com*.

Chapter 18

Not Midnite but 8 p. m. in Paris:
Beggars, Gypsies, Pickpockets and All

We were transported back 100 years when we visited Paris last year, a-la Woody Allen. 2020 back to 1920. Café Dupleix was located on Boulevard de Grennelle and not far from our hotel. As it was only one metro stop from us, we decided to walk in the cold Paris rain. Umbrella in hand, the maître-de sat us next to a couple of chaps, as is often the case in French cafes. Non, Je préfère m'asseoir de l'autre côté du restaurant, in my tourist French. What a fortunate decision to request sitting on the other side of the restaurant. Smack in the middle of its ambiance, near the bar, and with the outdoor tables through the window behind us. We sat relieved and comfortable. The waiter was probably in his early twenties and spoke English. Next to us were about a dozen middle-aged men sitting at a round make-shift table and having a grand ol' time. On the table were a few pitchers of beer and each gentleman holding a personal stein, drinking and talking in high spirit. "Sorry for all the noise," our waiter said. 'Pas du tout', not at all. But I wasn't sure, actually. We ordered, and shortly thereafter, they broke out in song. Incredible! Singing French folk songs together, acapella and just about everyone at Café Dupleix was being entertained for sure. Our humble American selves were sitting right next to them. Oblivious to us, they continued their jolly songs, and something cued them to change the format. Each one broke out in song individually, one after the other, and each one as good as the next. Clear and projecting voices, flawless in remembering lyrics as they appeared, none of the patrons blinked an eye to all of this, taking it all in stride. And each song was different, with no repeats. "Who are these people?" I asked the waiter. "They are farmers here from SW France near the Pyrenees, attending a national agricultural convention at their hotel," he said to us.

In reading Ernest Hemingway and his café culture escapades in his many books, he mentions how he and his friends would break out in song. A common cultural practice in those days, the 1920s. Well, there was no TV, no movies to attend to, and no computers and cell phones to distract. It is what they did, how they occupied and entertained themselves. I remember growing up in Brooklyn, New York, in the 1950s, when people would often break out in song in the streets by themselves. A case in point was my next-door neighbor, Melvin Portnoy. You knew it was 4 o'clock because that was when Melvin, of Jewish ethnicity, would be singing Domenico Modugno's "Volare" and Julius La Rosa's "Hey Cumpare" in Italian as he daily marched down the street coming home from school. How did he learn those lyrics?

Well, these guys in Paris were certainly comfortable in their ritual. Farmers and rural residents throughout history would commonly sing together and in groups, not just Ernest Hemingway and his Parisian buddies. Since they were from SW France, some of the songs were sung in Spanish. I surmised that border citizens in Spain would be bilingual. It was a treat!

We did take part in the Parisien cafe culture. My original intent in returning to Paris after 50 years was to sit along the Seine and discuss among the dead French philosophers the errors of their ways. I did all that and more. They left God out of the equation, so no real wisdom there. This was no surprise, but the resurgence of Catholicism in France was. Mass at St. Germain de Pres and St. Sulpice was SRO. And I have read that the Catholic resurgence is real. There is hope.

Switch to 'Le Bouillon Chartier', a Parisien classic. "Is this cabernet?" "Yes, this is Cabernet." The waiter abruptly replied. Hmm, not so sure. We ordered another carafe, this time Merlot. "Is this merlot?" "Yes, this is Merlot." The waiter abruptly replied again. Hmm; so weak, so tasteless. Was this the famous French wine so touted in American advertising and with an inviting rustic painting of its bottles hung on our living room wall in Florida? Well, this was the wine served to us at 'Le Bouillon Chartier,' one of Paris' most popular and antiquated restaurants, lines out the door after 8 pm. Going strong since 1896 and packed with over 300 patrons, the décor and the ambiance drew you into another era. Then the bread was dry, and we complained. He took it back and gave it to another table. LoL. Another standard in the 1920s, I guess. After reading 'A Moveable Feast,' Ernest Hemingway enlightened me about yet another Parisian practice of the 1920s, diluting carafes of wine with water. No wonder Hemingway, his wife, and friends could drink so much wine together. No wonder so tasteless. So happy to be there. We could not get upset and just laughed it off.

But I'm not so sure pickpockets are only a remnant of the 1920s. It is a lasting practice of the citizenry, especially in the crowded quarters of Le Metro. A group of 20-somethings trapped my darling wife in the corner on our first metro trip. It was obvious what they were doing to her. I thought it was just the crowded situation, but her screams proved it a clear situatifrewon of a pick pocketing attempt. "I know what you are doing; get away from me!" she yelled. I turned around, and they dispersed. No, pick-pocketing is common in Europe and any large city, really. My own uncle Carmine was a New York City pickpocket of the 1950s and 60s. Quick of hand and a master of distraction, they've got their games planned down to a 'T.' It didn't seem this attempt was so professional, though, and thus easily thwarted. But I did think we might have a fight on our hands. No, they escaped out and then into another car of Le Metro. We love Paris!

This article was edited from the original in Baglino, Michael J. 2022. *You Only Live Thrice*. Morris Publishing.

PHOTOS

Ave Maria, Florida

Columbia Restaurante, Tampa

Il Belaggio - W. Palm Bch., FL

Garvin Heights - Winona, MN

Stalin and Lenin, heroes of the Marxist left - lovely people.

Two College Wrestlers, Michael Sarah Baglino

Two real college wrestlers -
Michael Baglino and Larry Marchionda

Steve Ficara at Cresthaven Assisted Living, W. Palm Bch.

Michael Matone at Mar-a-Lago, Palm Beach

Clint Eastwood

Elton John

Rat Pack with Danny Devito [Lou Patavino]

Jackie Gleason

[Michael Walters]

Justin Timberlake?

Willie Nelson?

Carmine Baglino, Uncle Tuffy

AKA - Joe Matone, Sensational Brooklyn Welterweight

Saba, Melvin, and Family

Baglino's 2022 style

Part IV Politics and History

Chapter 19
Servant Leadership - Ron Desantis Style?

Though not an endorsement of Governor Ron Desantis as President, allow me to use some examples of his leadership and style to explain what is needed in dealing with our current social and political dilemma. Recent TV political advertisements presented the case for re-electing Florida Governor Ron Desantis. One such ad included a former U. S. Naval officer referring to Ron Desantis as a 'true servant leader.' Such an impressive, honorable comment and admirable qualities are spoken by one of his fellow Naval officers. It prompted me to seek out the characteristics of a 'true servant leader.'

Previous to serving as Governor of Florida, Ron Desantis graduated from Yale University and Harvard Law School. What strikes this author is his being captain of the Yale University Baseball Team. To me, always important - a regular guy. He was a Lieutenant in the U. S. Navy, deployed to Iraq, and advisor to Seal Team One. He earned the Bronze Star, Navy and Marine Corps Commendation Medal, Global War on Terrorism Service Medal, and Iraq Campaign Medal. He subsequently won election to Florida's 6th congressional district as a congressman before being elected Governor. That's it in a nutshell. And he and his family are practicing Roman Catholics.

Is he a servant leader? Does he have a vision of the future for Floridians? Can he inspire and lead its citizens? Do we know his core values through his communication and actions? Is he for us, and is it about us?

> **Proverbs 29: 18,** "Where there is no vision, the people perish; but he that keepeth the law, happy is he. "

The first test for a political leader is preparedness, and as Hurricane Ian approaches [at the time of this writing], it is being done. He made sure of it for each storm that has approached Florida since 2018. From there, our Governor initiated such policies as election reform and entrepreneurial education and training showing his preference for economic leadership and a free market as opposed to command economies. He instituted executive actions against threats posed by China, Cuba, Iran, Russia, North Korea, Syria, and Venezuela. These actions helped thwart cyber threats and real estate investments based on skeptical motives. He appointed trustees throughout our state university system, assuring higher educational integrity in terms of finance and propaganda. Recently the governor has stymied the left's poisonous public school curriculum agenda of gender theory and critical race theory. Desantis has made known his recognition of our principles and rights under siege by the left. And so he eliminated the Florida state university and college policies of 'diversity, equity and inclusion' as antithetical to democracy and American values. Further, he banned sex change procedures as health care procedures while at the same time signing the strongest pro-life bill in Florida history.

He's not a passive politician, and it is not just words. BLM and Antifa riots are not tolerated in Florida, sanctuary cities are banned, and Chinese Communist land grabs in its rural sector are opposed. Ahead of the game, Governor Desantis has made it known from the start that he favors freedom over control, especially government control, both personally and economically. He kept the schools open, the churches open, the businesses open, and the masks off. He maintains that our schools teach values in keeping with western democratic values and traditional Christian/Judeo values. Of course, the left starts calling names after successes like this. They have no argument. It is the governor of California who is the 'neo-fascist.' Theirs is a state of government control. Centralized control is the purpose of the left. Decentralization of power is their enemy. Opposition to the overturning of Roe vs. Wade is imperative for them, not only because of the abortion issue but because it brings these decisions out of the hands of the central government. This, to the left, is the solution to all problems as they see it. Fear of freedom and control is their motivation.

Proverbs 11: 3, "The integrity of the upright shall guide them: but the perverseness of transgressors shall destroy them."

Governor Desantis is a stickler for personal integrity. He sends illegals to Massachusetts, Washington, D. C., and New York because he knows Pres. Biden and these urban mayors are not. He confronts them, for they lean on federal policy and leftist political ideology, not themselves. It is called hypocrisy; their personal lives do not live their ideological beliefs.

Isaiah 41: 10, "Fear not, for I am with you; be not dismayed, for I am your God; I will strengthen you, I will help you, I will uphold you with my righteous right hand."

This is the leader attempting to get us back on track toward our rightful future. He is one of us too. He gets his strength from God, not Karl Marx. Recently before this writing, Desantis won the gubernatorial race by 20 points, a landslide. Why? Because Desantis won by his example, and the citizens of Florida love him. He has an awareness of the existential reality opposing political parties intend for this country. Servant leaders are grounded in reality. Hard work and willingness to sacrifice is his style. He's a fighter.

Source:

Perkins, Bill. 2000. *Awaken the Leader Within: How the Wisdom of Jesus can Unleash Your Potential.* Grand Rapids, Michigan: Zondervan Publishing House.

Chapter 20
Just What is that European Philosophy of Marxism Anyway?

European philosophy is making headway once again in America. Dialectical materialism, the dictatorship of the proletariat, capitalist ruling class, revolutionary working class, class conflict, bourgeoisie, classless society. These are all terms emanating from the Communist Manifesto, written by German social philosopher and economist Karl Marx. They are repeated every day in the halls of congress and in the mainstream media. Well, not those exact terms, just the concepts they are associated with. These terms all have negative connotations in America, so they will use words like progressive, working people, white privilege, the rich and wealthy, equity, exploitation, cultural appropriation, critical race theory, etc. All to help break down the standard cultural framework and economic structure. Marxism of the 21st century.

Karl Marx, a 19th-century philosopher, and economist, maintained that the history of the world was a history of class struggle. That is, the Marxist theory (adopted as the official philosophy of the Soviets, China, and other communist countries) is that political and historical events result from the conflict of social forces and are interpreted as a series of contradictions and their solutions. The conflict is to be caused by material needs. He referred to this theory as 'dialectical materialism.' As material needs changed, so did the social and economic structure of society. Follow me here.

"The history of the world is
the history of class struggle."
COMMUNISM[future centuries]
CAPITALISM [18th century and beyond]
FEUDALISM [middle ages]
SLAVERY [pre-middle ages]

Each stage in history is based on the control of one class over the other, an exploitive relationship. The existing contradiction is described as a thesis versus an antithesis. Thus, slavery being an illogical institution, will leave the majority of people in material need. Though slave owners reap the benefits of their control [thesis], slaves are naturally opposed to this relationship of powerlessness and material want [antithesis]. Conflicts emerge, and a new social order develops [synthesis]. That new social order, according to Marx, becomes feudalism.

Feudalism is the next stage in history whereby large landholders, lords, and nobles maintain control over their workers, serfs, for a meager wage. Not quite slavery but exploitive nonetheless. Pre-industrialized Europe, Latin America, and post-slavery Brazil and America are examples. Again the contradictions of this relationship reach their boiling point as serfs and indentured servants cannot improve their lot materially. Conflicts between land owners, servants, and serfs arise to the point of social change once again, as the existing relationships will not function. Combining this with a worldwide industrial revolution, forces are in play for new relationships to emerge. This new system is called capitalism.

Capitalism is the system emerging in Europe and the United States especially. These two continents proceeded with industrial growth and wealth based on the capitalist ruling class dominating over their workers or the working class. Another way in which Marx referred to this relationship is the owners of the means of production's exploitive control over the proletariat. The bourgeoisie is the middle class and small business owners who actually imitate the culture of the capitalist ruling class to help maintain the former's control. They live in better neighborhoods, join the local country clubs, and send their children to better schools. The mass of workers, however, fuels their economic growth and wealth through their hard work while they remain relatively poor, just getting by. The only solution is the uniting of all workers, mostly through union organization and revolt against the ruling class. Through violent revolution, they take control of all property and business, emerging into a worker's paradise.

Capitalist ruling class

______________________________= violent revolution

Proletariat working class

Sounds simple. It has never occurred in history. Rather, communist revolutions have only occurred in agrarian economies, those that have never developed industrially. Eventually, as hopefully, these nations do develop, the growth of a centralized government keeps control, and the workers maintain its cooperative management of all business and industry. Marx envisioned communist revolutions in advanced capitalist nations like Europe and the United States. A dictatorship would soon emerge, called 'the dictatorship of the proletariat.' It would last for a mere 20 years as the state eventually withers away. Large centralized bureaucratic governments are entrenched and do not wither away. Democrats know this, and their increased budgeting of ever more government programs makes sure the centralized state is expanded. Here in the United States, since the unions have not emerged as the leaders of the revolution, leftism has become more of an intellectual challenge. The intelligentsia, along with governmental bureaucracy, have joined forces over both capitalists and workers by imposing their way. Through university training and media control, the message is getting out there. Joining forces with the centralized federal bureaucracy, their march continues.

Why is it imposed? Because Marx left a few things out. He did not foresee working people themselves owning stock in private businesses and corporations and sharing wealth. He did not foresee professional athletes such as NBA, NFL, MLB, and MLS ball players earning millions through the free market. He did not foresee the professional class growing in general and the working classes living as comfortably as they do. So the media skews the perception. He did not foresee religion, especially Christianity continuing to make such a strong impact on western culture and around the world. He did not foresee God working in this world and race relations improving to the point of Christian brotherhood. So, they have to create more racial strife [see ch. 7]. To Marx, Christianity was the enemy, and all leftist forces attempted to destroy it. Christians owe their allegiance to God, not the state. Communists cannot have this. Leftists exacerbate ongoing racial and ethnic strife and believe such brotherhood must only exist within the socialist social structure, none other. It is all about power, and this ideology is their god, not the Father, the Son, and the Holy Spirit.

Marx believed the history of the world is a history of class struggle by finally bringing all classes into one classless society. Make everyone the same, and think the same within the centralized state [equity]. Capitalists believe that the history of the world is a history of freeing the means of production toward growth and material abundance. Christianity believes that the history of the world is to lead man up toward God with God in control. Your choice. But let me remind you, all societies without God are destined for failure.

Source:

Dr. Baglino top of my head college lecture, or look up *The Communist Manifesto* by Karl Marx for yourself.

Part V Psychology and Religion

Chapter 21
Contemporary Theories on Behavior

The God of the Bible hates murmuring.

Philippians 2:13-15 For God is working in you, giving you the desire and the power to do what pleases him. Do everything without
complaining and arguing so that no one can criticize you. Live clean, innocent lives as children of God, shining like bright lights in a world full of crooked and perverse people.

Romans 8:28 "And we know that for those who love God, all things work together for good, for those who are called according to his purpose."

What are the most popular ways to explain behavior today? Well, identity politics focuses on sociocultural perspectives. The current growth in artificial intelligence and neurological psychology leans toward a more cognitive approach. Then there is Marxism, more sociological than psychological, and, unfortunately, regaining support in the academic world. Too much support.

Recently my wife and I received an invitation to a typical wedding in Miami. The groom was from Puerto Rico, and the bride was from Brazil. He was an American high school teacher [at Miami's 'American High School' BTW] who was accustomed to the daily schedule of the education world. I never found out her occupation, and not sure she was into a career, actually. Word was she was just looking for and American husband to help remain in the U. S. The wedding was scheduled at 1 PM on a Saturday. We were so looking forward to it, and since we had some difficulties getting ready that day, we were a little anxious that it was taking us so long. Finally, we made it to the church with about 5 minutes to spare. I wanted to arrive early, but at least we made it.

The parking lot was empty. Alarmed, I said to my wife, "Oh man, are we at the right church? Check the address." "This is the address," she replied. A gentleman walking on church grounds approached us. He turned out to be a church official. "Is there a wedding here today?" I asked. "Yes, you're at the right place." he quickly responded. "C'mon in."

We entered the church, and not a soul was in there. By now, it was past 1 PM. We looked at each other dumbfounded. "What's going on?" we said to each other. At 1:14, somebody else showed up, then at 1:20, a few more. By 1:30, the pews may have been 1/3 full. Our groom's friend arrived at 1:40. He was happy. More trickling in as time went by, and full by 3 PM. A lot of socializing and chattering. Nobody blinked an eye, and all seemed content with the entire afternoon. The bride showed up at 4. The groom was calm, with no anxieties, and the attendants settled in for the event. We went with it all. It was a lovely day.

To me, being late is disrespectful and inconsiderate. My daughter is always at least a half hour late. The groom didn't mind. The church attendants didn't seem to care. The bride certainly was OK with it all. Why? She was from Brazil, that's why. Punctuality is not a favored behavior among Brazilians, and though our Puerto Rican friend was never on time himself in our interactions, it wasn't as extreme. He knew it would happen and adjusted. A tolerance granted to his South American wife. What I have learned since is that in Brazil, the person with a higher status is granted the privilege of arriving later. I'm not sure, but I might have been searching for a second wife by 2 o'clock.

Cultural behaviors are based on shared beliefs, values, behavior patterns, and traditions. Those sharing these behaviors may be nations, ethnic groups, or communities of all types. The members are socialized to learn so. Arabs stand close to each other when talking, Europeans and Americans less so; we need our space. Cross-cultural research describes the continuum of culture based on the degree of individualism versus collectivism. Asians are collectivist in that the group, the family, and the community maintains dominance. Westerners are individualistic, where personal independence is the norm. African Americans can be quite collectivist in family and community and racial loyalties. WASPS can be quite individualistic and entrepreneurial. Personal goals versus group goals are the contrasting emphasis. In Japan, "the nail that stands out gets pounded down." In America, "the squeaky wheel gets the grease."

Cognitive theories emphasize perception based on biology, genetics, and mental processes. Mental processes mean how the brain works. This includes perception in social matters, memory, language, problem-solving, reasoning, and judgments. This approach to understanding behavior is useful in education and clinics. Sometimes our biological makeup can effect our perceptions and consequential behaviors. I am reminded of an extreme case illustrated in a recent re-run of an episode of "House," the popular TV series. Here the medical diagnosticians were treating an artist who had painted an obvious distortion of a model's face. It was biologically based - a neurological brain interference.

The growing field of artificial intelligence recognizes the parallels between the human mind and computers. Computers perform tasks as efficiently and similarly as our brains. This may include the logic of chess, the use of language, or even decision-making. All cognition.

Our brain works differently and perceives differently as we grow. Jean Piaget was the most influential child psychologist of the 20th century. His research led the way to our more detailed understanding of cognition. So let me outline a surface understanding. It is proven that cognitive growth proceeds as our brain develops. Firstly, brain communication with our muscular and skeletal systems allows for the development of coordination, senses, and motor skills. Reaching, touching, feeling, and grasping are all available now during infancy. Holding on to toys, sucking one's toes, and reaching for colored items. As toddlers, children learn how to talk and understand language. It is called symbolic thinking. Grades schoolers develop logic, comprehend ideas and figure numbers. Teenagers think abstractly and understand the concepts of politics, ethics, and morality.

It is during adulthood when our modern murmurs come into being. Taught to be mindful, sober, and alert are the desired lessons. In a Christian sense, to depart from the focus on God and the things of God brings on a murmuring that battles with the uncertainty of reality. We call that cognitive biases and distortions. This is the sort of view that "life is awful, it is so full of reality" syndrome, and determining reality are the things of God: mindfulness, sobriety, and alertness from both sides of the brain.

Perceptual biases and distortions, lack of attention and concentration, and memory retrieval are all adult cognitive processes to allow for the penetration of reality into our consciousness. Do we think like everyone else and join the bandwagon, or can we assess the truth even if it does not conform to the group? That's the body-snatcher syndrome of group think. Do we blame others for our failures but pat ourselves on the back for our own successes? Do we stereotype and categorize others with judgment attached? All Irish drink, all Italians have mafia connections, and all Chinese own laundries. Do black faces or European faces look more distinctive, or does everyone look the same in each race?

Ever taken a job, and it was not what was expected? You romanticize about helping the poor, and the working conditions are a little too much to handle, perhaps. A priest asked me to work and live with him in a Central American barrio for the summer. I knew better for myself and joked that I'd stay at the local Holiday Inn and commute. You want to work in the inner city, but the violence and lack of personal dignity everywhere make you ponder if it is worth it. This is cognitive dissonance, and we are called to assess reality for ourselves - can we adjust, or should we leave? It didn't fit into my original perceptions of the matter.

The other popular theory to explain behavior is Marxism, a sociological and philosophical construct, and to this author, a collective bias and distortion of reality, otherwise called a collective mental derangement. Economics and the material world are its focus. Karl Marx focused on the economic conflict between workers and owners of the means of production and called it dialectic materialism. Marx believed all of world history was a history of material want and class struggle between these groups. God and religion were in their way. He despised religion, especially Judaism, Catholicism, and the Lutheran Church. The 'opiate of the people' was his mantra about religion. Since the history of the world is a history of class struggle, the socio-economic class an individual finds himself in will determine his behavior. And his behavior was to struggle to free himself from the shackles of capitalism, take control of this economic system, and refrain from copying the lifestyle of the rich and famous. Dress down, create alternative lifestyles, and oppose Western morality. This movement is to create a world of equality and equity according to the Chinese Communist Party mode. At least, that is what Marxism has transformed itself to be in the 2020s. It is imposed upon our students and the employed cogs in the technological/ industrial/ governmental complex. Once the military is conquered from within, watch out. One universal class, equitable, compliant, and controlled by the administrative state.

They believe it is destiny and wants to force us to do it. It's the politics of envy and deviance. These people murmur a lot, sometimes very loudly.

Romans 12:2 "Do not be conformed to this world, but be transformed by the renewal of your mind, that by testing you may discern what is the will of God, what is good and acceptable and perfect."

Source:

Berk, Laura. *Exploring Lifespan Development*. New York: Pearson Education, 2018.

Matlin, Margaret W. *Cognition, 8th ed.* Hoboken, NJ: Wiley, 2013.

Taylor, Shelley E. et al. *Social Psychology*. Upper Saddle River, NJ: Pearson Prentice Hall, 2006.

Chapter 22
Spiritual Combat: Scupoli and Robinson

From the cover of *Spiritual Combat Revisited*:

"This indeed is the hardest of all struggles: for while we strive against self, self is striving against us, and therefore is the victory here most glorious and precious in the sight of God."

Lorenzo Scupoli (*The Spiritual Combat*)

Nothing new here. It's been all said before. Apostles repeat the truth: this is a world of spiritual combat.

Ephesians 6:12 "For we do not wrestle against flesh and blood, but against the rulers, against the authorities, against the cosmic powers over this present darkness, against the spiritual forces of evil in the heavenly places."

First published in 1589, *The Spiritual Combat* by Lorenzo Scupoli has become a great spiritual classic of Catholic thought. To become one spirit with God, says Scupoli, one must recognize the true and perfect spiritual life. That is the recognition of the four battles of spiritual combat: distrust of self, trust of God, spiritual exercises, and prayer.

1. Distrust of Self

Proverbs 3: 5-6 "Trust in the LORD with all your heart and lean not on your own understanding; in all your ways submit to him, and he will make your paths straight."

Scupoli exhorts that though we strive toward perfection to love and serve the Lord, though we seek the goodness and greatness of God, we must also acknowledge our own nothingness. Mortification of our selves then becomes our goal, eliminating our appetites and desires in order to prepare ourselves for the battle. We must annihilate our will in all things in order to win the battle. Only the brave warriors in Christ will receive the crown, no distractions.

2. Trust in God

But self-distrust is not enough to win our battles, but rather a perfect trust in God. This is not only maintaining confidence in God, but we are required to call to mind Holy Scripture so as never to be confused. So recognition of our own weakness must precede the recognition of God's omnipotence. Both together are necessary to precede all actions. By being distrustful of self and confident in God, by detesting one's own faults and passions, an individual will continue resolutely depending on God, not self.

Joshua 1:9 "Have I not commanded you? Be strong and courageous. Do not be frightened, and do not be dismayed, for the LORD your God is with you wherever you go."

3. **Spiritual Exercises**

Spiritual exercises involve the focus upon Him and Him crucified. The focus on God requires being free from other affections, from unnecessary curiosity. Way back when, in the year 1589, Scupoli noted that in our struggles, even the news of the world should be rejected and driven from us. Tell that to CNN and Fox, etc. As it is throughout scripture, the Book of Ecclesiastes originally tells us it is all vanity and entertainment. In the end, it is to know, love, and serve the Lord, fear God, and keep his commandments, for the world will pass us by, and only God's judgment will prevail.

Scupoli warns us that the most dangerous inhibitor toward focusing on God is the obstinance of pride. He continues that the prideful will not submit to other opinions and judgments no matter their worthiness. Tell that to the world's politicians. To counteract, become the fool for the love of God, and we shall be wiser than Solomon. Exercising ourselves to please God alone becomes plain and easy by practice. Exercise toward victory over self and toward more confidence in God. For the Catholic Church, it is those anchors of attending mass, the Holy Eucharist, Cross of Christ, confession, and the Holy Rosary which summons all exercise in focusing on God.

Finally, it is exercising the call upon the Holy Spirit to light our paths, face all problems, to attain our goals. The spirit of truth and fear of the Lord brings us the wisdom needed for battle. The Holy Spirit helps us in our personal weakness, interceding for us and aiding in our focus and love of God.

4. **Prayer**

Pray is the instrument for the obtaining of graces flowing down from the source of all love and goodness. It is through prayer that God will fight and conquer for us. Prayer includes the praise of God, the earnest desire to serve God, the confidence that God will supply all that is needed for His service, and the continued commitment to remain steadfast and joyful in submitting to His Divine Providence. This is for us to elevate our hearts and minds to the Lord and meditate on some features of his life. And aside from prayer and taking of the Holy Eucharist at mass, it is the Blessed Virgin and all the saints whose torments for the love of Him will aid us in our spiritual battle, in our focus, and for our spiritual and temporal necessities. The Rosary is key in focusing on the life of Christ.

This is but a brief summary of Scupoli's treatise on spiritual warfare. An in-depth account of his classic will bring further understanding of the role of the above anchors of Christianity and Catholicism in particular. It will illuminate the sufferings of Jesus and what that suffering did for our own souls. Consequently, it will illuminate what we should do for Jesus.

Luke 10:19 Behold, I give unto you power to tread on serpents and scorpions, and over all the power of the enemy: and nothing shall by any means hurt you."

Sources:

Robinson, Jonathan. *Spiritual "Combat Revisited.* San Francisco: Ignatius Press.

Scupoli, Dom Lorenzo. 1992. *Combattimento Spirituale.* Milan: Edizione Paolini.

Chapter 23
Noam Chomsky and Cognitive Behavioral Therapy

Isn't it interesting how totally opposite interpretations of social and political events exist and even create an explosive confrontation? This has been the way of things in current American politics for the past 50 or more years and getting more extreme. So, each side calls the other extremist and tries to paint the other side as such, a gaslighting effect. Current issues include the economy, inflation, unemployment, the border, crime, health care, etc.

Noam Chomsky has been a superstar in the field of anthropology, cognition, and linguistics for some 50 years. He is clearly a left-leaning intellectual, though it really makes no difference as to his accounts of why individuals might misunderstand, miscommunicate and misinterpret events as they happen. Aside from the philosophical underpinnings, values, and beliefs each person carries with him/herself definitely affect differences in perception of matters. Chomsky points out there are mental filters that allow our minds to see only certain parts of the event, thus contributing to our disagreements.

We distort our memories, values, and beliefs by deleting a lot of information. For example, we might not hear traffic while driving because we are listening to the radio. It's there but

somehow ignored. We create our own understanding of a
situation based on what we take in, not entirely of what is there.
While driving, the guy in front of us is an idiot for going too slow,
and the guy behind us is a moron for tailgating. Likewise, the guy
behind us calls us an idiot, while the fellow behind him is a moron,
and so on. We don't see the whole picture. Psychologically
Chomsky calls these deletions of all the available information as
mental filtering. These mental filters include generalizations,
deletions, and distortions, and in order to see the event or
situation clearly, we need to be made aware in spite of ourselves.
I guess you can call that education. Clients in the counseling
situation are confronted with a counselor who helps in this effort;
it is a form of cognitive behavioral therapy [CBT].

Generalizations

Ever get dumped or betrayed by a friend? It becomes so easy
to say 'no such thing as true friends' or 'You just can't trust
women.' A generalization is a universal truth and places things in
categories: the good, the bad, the ugly, the rich, and the poor. So,
everything falls into place, 'all men are rotten,' and 'all women are
deceitful.' Robbed in the city, all Puerto Ricans then become
thieves and all Italians hoodlums. If bitten by a dog, then all dogs
are dangerous. A phobia develops.

Deletions

Deletions occur when we concentrate on a specific task. When we focus, we delete most of the data that reaches our brain. Too many details and excessive information can distract us from our task, and so it is gone from our minds. It is necessary to accomplish our task and a natural instinct. But sometimes, we elicit the opposite response, and this is called tunnel vision. Ever perform on stage in a play or musical show? Revues are great. An admirable performance, according to the audience. But there is always one who just didn't see it that way, and that is the one you remember. That is focusing on the negative aspects of situations and deleting the positive. It deflates our ego and unnecessarily so.

Distortions

"My neighbor didn't say hello this morning. He must be angry at me." No, he was depressed because he was diagnosed with a disease. Misinterpreting reality is so common when we do not have all the information at hand. We sometimes will see things that do not actually exist. Or we may distort by black and white thinking, all or nothing at all with no grays in between. It is a matter of extremes.

I particularly like the distorted thinking of a 'heavens reward fallacy,' being Catholic and all that. It is the belief that as one struggles and suffers, there is a just reward at the end of the line. Sometimes hard work and sacrifice don't pay off, and we won't achieve what we set out to achieve. And when that reward doesn't arrive, we may experience anger, frustration, and depression. Oh well, that may be in this life time. This is one to think about. Life ain't fair. The bible has a few things to say about a 'heavens reward,' but not as in Noam Chomsky's book, I guess. Just one more example of the need for combining cognitive behavioral therapy and the Christian faith.

James 1:12 "Blessed is the man who remains steadfast under trial, for when he has stood the test he will receive the crown of life, which God has promised to those who love him."

Matthew 6:6 "But when you pray, go into your room and shut the door and pray to your Father who is in secret. And your Father who sees in secret will reward you."

I don't know if Chomsky knows this one below. It's political.

Revelation 2:26 "The one who conquers and who keeps my works until the end, to him I will give authority over the nations."

No real conclusions about politics here, just a summary of how our thinking can distort and skew reality, and we are all subject to it. And I give homage to and consider Chomsky one of the original contributors to CBT, Marxist or not.

Source:

Ramsay, Kain. 2018. *Noam Chomsky's Mental   Filters.* Strategic Life Coaching.

Chapter 24
Warning Against Prejudice

I wrote and published this article in the monthly Christian magazine '*The Upper Room*' sometime in the early 1990s when living in Miami. I asked them to retrieve it but to no avail. They could not find the article, so there is officially no record of it. So, I reprint it here; sure, they won't mind after all that. It's mine, anyway.

James 2: 1 My brothers, as believers in our Lord Jesus Christ, the Lord of Glory, you must never treat people in different ways according to their outward appearance.

Miami is truly a multicultural and multiracial community with a wide range of classes and incomes. As a member of an interracial family, we are well aware of the need to treat all individuals the same. However, even we need reminders from time to time, given the enormous diversity of cultures that live here.

On a four-day holiday weekend, our extended family visited southern, rural Georgia for a family reunion. All of my wife's relatives were born and lived in this little agricultural village whose economy revolved around cotton, peanut, and vegetable farms. From a privileged middle-class urban environment, we found ourselves in a poor, rural community. We had a wonderful time of southern hospitality, food, song, and dance. As one of a few white persons among several hundred, it once again struck me how similar we all are. The greetings, conversations, laughter, party enthusiasm, individual concerns, and planning of this reunion were no different from any other family and social gathering I have attended.

What is it that divides races and cultures in our society? Why can't people socialize from a perspective of equality, belonging, and comfort? Whatever the social and political basis for such divisions, I believe, as does James, that obeying the law of the Kingdom as found in scripture is the solution. "Love your neighbor as you love yourself." But if you treat people according to their outward appearance, you are guilty of sin, and God's Law condemns you as a lawbreaker. Ultimately, it is our common beliefs and behavior within the Kingdom that unifies us in the body of Christ.

PRAYER: Gracious and loving God, remind us of the need to behave according to Christian principles and treat others, regardless of racial and cultural background as our brothers.

THOUGHT FOR THE DAY: True unity in a culturally diverse society comes from loving God and obeying His commandments. Focus: inner-city communities.

Chapter 25
You Got Anxiety? Bio/Psycho/Social Factors

Worried about the future? Over eat or under eat? Irritable at times? Get headaches or belly aches? Avoid or sit out of social activities? Can't focus? Well, this is another one of my favorite lectures in psychology class. Why so? Seems college students today have a lot of anxiety. And though some anxiety may be good for you, spurring on growth, for the most part, it may cause a myriad of symptoms and consequent health issues. They are glued to their desks when I talk about it.

It's that inner discomfort or nervousness we all experience from our precarious world, our rushed life. It might manifest itself through problems with friends and family, financial concerns, and speaking before others, especially formally in a group. As Charlie Brown once said, though we might want it so, life is not a spiritual jet stream.

We can analyze anxiety through its classic bio/psycho/social components, that is, biological, psychological, and sociological factors. Some are prone to anxiety because of certain amounts of chemicals in the body [biological]. Popular psychologist Jordan Peterson points out that when lobsters win their battles at the bottom of the ocean, their bodies secrete more serotonin and experience a general state of comfort and well-being. They start to prance and dance around the ocean floor. The same is true with humans. Coping and success in life is a natural sedative and yet euphoric experience.

Genetic dispositions can contribute to anxiety, and family medical history is known to be an indicator of the same. Minor illnesses might result, such as dizziness, high blood pressure, digestive disorders, muscle tension, and fatigue. Of course, prolonged anxiety can lead to much worse.

Psychological experiences from childhood learned fears and past traumatic experiences could trigger it [war, child abuse]. And then if one is more prone to anxiety through pessimistic thinking and other cognitive components such as worry, fear, loss of control, paranoia, panic, irritability, and restlessness. Individuals respond in one of three ways - flee from a situation, freeze up, or engage in overly aggressive behavior. Through family conflict, for example, an individual might run away or hide in a room, be passive and say nothing, or lash out with anger. But it takes prayer and lots of it.

Philippians 4:6 "do not be anxious about anything, but in everything by prayer and supplication with thanksgiving let your requests be made known to God."

Culture and socialization can affect anxiety-prone. Gender differences in social situations may bring on anxious feelings through perception. Some situations may bring up survival instincts. Do I belong? Do I fit in? Why so uncomfortable? Women are more open about it, while men are less likely to acknowledge or report anxiety. Our modern bureaucratic, technological society engenders anxiety through its tendency toward control. It is that anti-human experience that will bring it on. The dilemma of the day, that is, the unhumanistic authoritarian impulse brought on by both ideology and the bureaucratic/ technological state.

> **Romans 8:15** "For you did not receive the spirit of slavery to fall back into fear, but you have received the Spirit of adoption as sons, by whom we cry, "Abba! Father!""

Finally, humanistic and positive psychology, originated by the likes of Carl Rogers and Abraham Maslow, proposes that our own egos and anxiety are intertwined. Referred to as transactional analysis, an individual leads an existence of carrying around three egos or selves within the ideal, real, and perceived self, that ever-evolving self-concept. An imbalanced self-concept would then lead to social anxiety disorder. So that when two people meet, it is then three egos each or six individuals interacting. LoL. "Who am I? Who are you?" they say subconsciously. Former rock stars and celebrities Jimi Hendrix and Janis Joplin were their ideal selves on stage. It became too difficult for them to deal with every day coping responsibilities and reconcile the two selves. It lead to a faulty perception of who they really were and further to an intolerable anxiety - incongruent selves. Drugs were the answer; death was the result.

Popular author, TV, and radio evangelist Joyce Meyer maintain in many of her books and sermons that we must learn to handle fear, worry, and anxiety in a Godly way. We start by saying, "I trust God." It releases His power to work in our lives. When troubled by anxiety, she calls us to study God's Word and remember what He has done for us before. Then remove the words fear and worry from your vocabulary.

> **Psalm 34: 4** " I sought the Lord and He answered me. And delivered me from all my fears."

So, though not intended at the onset of this article, this author would be remiss if he did not mention some self-treatment steps when in the midst of or even before any onset of anxious feelings.

1. Maintain a positive attitude through prayer and meditation;

2. Sleep well, 8 hours at least;

3. Exercise, walk, swim, stretch, and participate in golf and other social sports;

4. Get away from salt, sugar, caffeine, alcohol, and nicotine;

5. Eat more fruits and vegetables, avoid junk food;

6. Know what it is that brings on your personal anxiety;

7. Discuss with a confidant, husband, wife, or friend.

Proverbs 3: 5-6 "Trust in the Lord with all your heart and lean not on your own understanding; in all your ways submit to him, and he will make your paths straight."

Source:

Pastorino, Ellen and Doyle Portillo. 2019. *What is Psychology?*

Foundations, Applications and Integration. Boston: Cengage

Chapter 26
Psychology or Christianity?

There certainly are many successful and influential psychologists out there, each with his/her own perspective and approach. Psychology, the scientific study of cognition and behavior, is growing in the fields of education, clinical and counseling, health and sports, and industrial and organizational psychology. These are but a few. Their focuses vary from biology, cognition, learning, behavior, and culture to humanistic perspectives. Common to each field is the suggestion that behavior is improved through a varying emphasis on learning from example, by encouragement, by a better environment, through education, and of course, today's prescriptions, biological psychology. All are worthy approaches. This author maintains that along with Christ and Christianity as the major focus, you've got something both personally and culturally penetrating and profound as a behavioral discipline. Christianity is the best behavioral approach, and along with scientific and proven practices in psychology over the past 100 years, we have an especially effective discipline here.

Let's take a look.

A. Example

Role Modeling is what psychologists mean by example. Tony Robbins, a popular motivational speaker promoting growth psychology, maintains that modeling is learning through copying the behavior of another. Further, he states it is changing your behavior to improve your mindset and achieve your goals. It is becoming more of who you are through copying a role model. This writer has been a church lecturer for 45 years. He began while sitting in his regular pew one Sunday in 1977 and observing a church lecturer who happened to be a news anchor on the local Miami CBS news. "I can do that," I said to myself shortly after I volunteered to lector at our church, and I have been volunteering ever since. These are other common examples.

Parents can be effective role models. Children will copy the positive behavior patterns of their parents. This may include diet, dress, exercise, attending church, prayer, controlling temper, reading, participating in fun activities, loving their mates and children, and a myriad of other behaviors. Of course, children can often model drinking, anger, indifference, laziness, etc.

Professionalism in the workplace can be modeled to fellow workers. Work ethic, dress, communication styles, honesty and ethics, demeanor, and poise, in general, are all admirable employee qualities. And, of course, role models can be either supervisors or the general culture of the workplace exhibited by associates.

In counseling psychology, modeling is often used to convey the better or more proper behavior expected of a client. Again, we learn our behaviors through example.

And what of Christianity? Mother Angelica, the founder of Eternal Word Television Network, points out that Jesus Christ, who shows us how to act and react under any circumstance, is our perfect role model. As heirs to the throne of God, we are to be gods through the love of our Lord Jesus Christ. And our love of Jesus would make us want to be like Him. We are to change the qualities of the soul and resemble Jesus in many ways so that we can glorify both Him and the Father for all eternity. Thus our goal in this life is to be a perfect image of Jesus as Jesus is the perfect image of the Father.

What do we imitate? Loyalty, zeal, nobility, and loving qualities. We do this through an ongoing quest for knowledge of Him and prayer, a way of life. We do this through following Jesus by praying daily and behaving accordingly as he expects of us. He'll let us know how. So it takes faith.

Matthew 11:29 "Take My yoke upon you and learn from Me, for I am gentle and humble in heart, and you will find rest for your souls."

1 Timothy 4:12 Don't let anyone think less of you because you are young. Be an example to all believers in what you say, in the way you live, in your love, your faith, and your purity.

B. Encouragement

Psychologically speaking, encouragement is communicating to someone with the intent of instilling a more desired behavior. This may be courage, perseverance, confidence, inspiration, or hope in a challenging situation. Communication may also be used to help an individual realize a potential. Encouragement can include something as simple as listening or having patience with an individual. A smile or comforting words can encourage. On the other end, involving oneself with another is an encouraging gesture, such as an act of kindness or working together on a project. You can convey the need to hang in there, recognize accomplishments, and inspire others to reach goals. It's catching.

A scientific approach in psychology to encourage is what is referred to as 'positive reinforcement.' Positive reinforcement is a concept originated by famed learning psychologist B. F. Skinner.

This concept is a basic principle of Skinner's operant conditioning, which states that introducing a desirable or pleasant stimulus after a behavior, such as a reward, will increase a desired behavior again. In other words, this desirable stimulus is intended to reinforce the behavior, making it more likely that the behavior will occur in the future.

Common examples of positive reinforcement may include giving a gold star to a child in 1st grade after he read a page in a book to the class. This will encourage the student to continue reading. Verbal praise or a pat on the back of a baseball player by the coach will encourage him to keep up the good work. He is appreciated. A supervisor may assign an employee a financial bonus for good work or hand out plaques of achievement as an employee of the month. Taking the kids out for ice cream or a movie is a good reward for properly behaving children at home.

Encouragement, in a Christian sense, is spiritual in that it is the Holy Spirit working within them. It is the indwelling Holy Spirit encouraging and helping the believer showing it is due to His workings. Also, fellow believers are called to encourage each other, that mutual support rooted in the way of Christ. Thus encouragement is also Christ-centered. It is Christ who comforts, guides, and instructs us toward victories. Through mutual support, we are built up. Rather than criticizing, shaming, judging, or mocking, we can be encouraged toward our goals through our Christ-centered efforts of unity, sympathy, and brotherly love. With God, all things are possible, especially in a community of Christians.

Joshua 1:9 "Have I not commanded you? Be strong and courageous. Do not be frightened, and do not be dismayed, for the Lord your God is with you wherever you go."

2 Timothy 1:7 For God gave us a spirit not of fear but of power and love and self-control.

Philippians 4:13 "I can do all things through him who strengthens me."

C. Environment

Psychology will tell you that human behavior is attributed to both dispositional and situational factors. Behavior is dispositional in that it originates from within the individual; it is internal. Perhaps an attitude exists, allowing a tendency to behave in a certain way. This may result from an individual's personality trait or genetic makeup. Biological conditions may precipitate a behavior such as hunger, chemical balance or imbalances, fatigue, drugs, and creating mood or feeling. The social situation or circumstance a person experiences and that circumstance's influencing behavior is referred to as situational factors; it is external. Perhaps the people with whom he/she is interacting will influence a particular behavior. Or perhaps it is the social structure found on the job, in the school, in the neighborhood.; that is, the environment. Rigid, authoritarian, laissez-faire, or democratic organizations affect behavior.

One famous psychological experiment is the Solomon Asch conformity experiment of the 1950s. Here a person's own opinions were influenced by those of a group. People were willing to ignore reality and give an incorrect answer in order to conform to the rest of the group. It depended on the level of group pressure, the size of the group, and the status of the group.

Current psychology focusing on situational factors points to American psychologist Urie Bronfenbrenner's ecological systems theory on child development. It is more of a social psychology. Human development is actually a complex system of relationships within the surrounding environment. And the environment is structured on many levels. The infographics below diagram these levels ranging from family influence to income, schools, government agencies, ideologies, and social changes during the times of development.

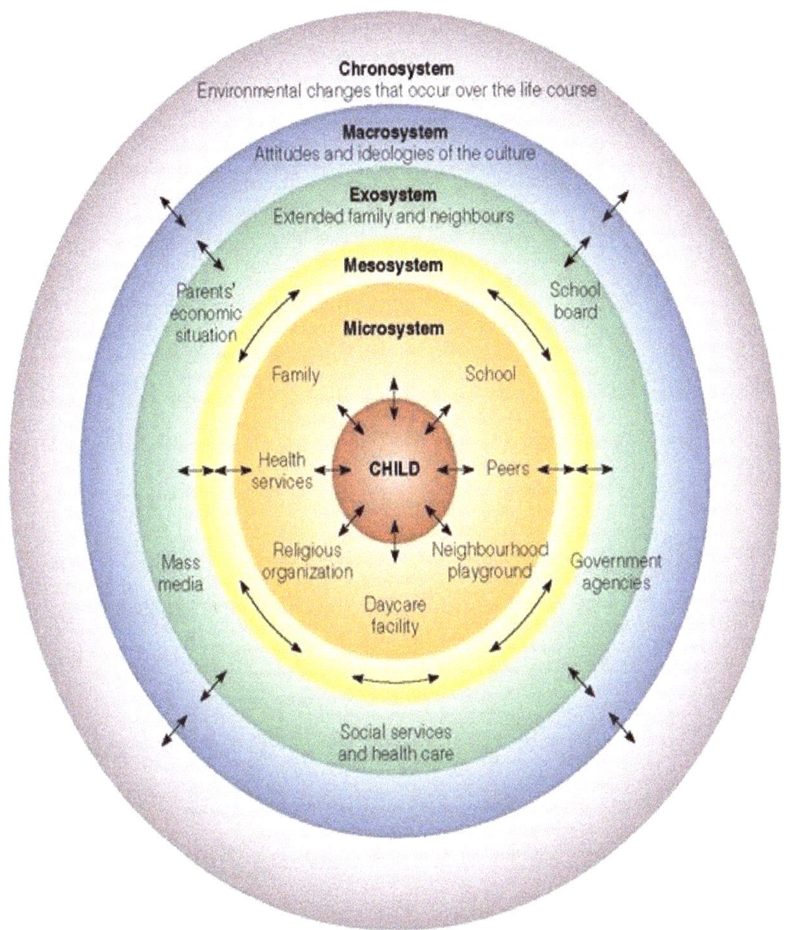

Pinterest

All levels have their influence in one way or another. It appears on the surface that the psychology of environmental influence is not in harmony with Christianity. Christianity focuses on human will, the choices people make during their lifetime in each and every situation. It asks humans to conform to the will of God to be more Christ-like. It is to persevere, decide and endure regardless of the situation.

Let us look at the Catholic view from renowned theologian Archbishop Fulton J. Sheen. Primarily, the Roman Catholic is to have goals, direction, and purpose, for if not, he would be pushed around by every wind there is, the external. This would be necessary throughout all stages of life, youth, adulthood, and the senior years. Through these stages, spirituality, rather than the flesh, power, or avarice, is paramount in decision-making and process. Spiritual dispositions overcome the seven deadly sins. A Catholic must rely on reason and will in that regard and not on instinct or impulse. Thus, he is talking about dispositional factors.

Life is determined by committing to ideals, purpose, and direction rather than the subconscious [lust, gluttony, greed, sloth, wrath, envy, and pride]. If not, the guilt of not admitting one's sins will give in to the lower instincts, along with overpowering reason and will. Sexual desires and scapegoating, for example, do not lead to fulfillment - but rather direction and purpose. We outgrow that. It is through our devotion to and walks with Christ that we then find our true identity and fulfillment. We rid ourselves of our sin and shame and our masks, admitting who we really are. Then we can grow. Our conflict is body and soul, matter and spirit, a battle to destroy one's egotism. Thus

Archbishop Sheen's view of Catholic psychology seems to align with humanistic or positive psychology. It is existential.

So, there is some common ground between psychology and Christianity. Growth or positive psychology has some parallels. However, it is the reliance on Christ that is needed for every situation in life, not the other way around. The new priests of the Western world, psychologists, and sociologists all emphasize the environment in determining behavior. The Marxist approach is the overreaching social structure, and so to improve behavior is to improve the social structure, ie. Social engineering. Poverty causes crime, not disobeying commandments. Social hierarchy causes prejudice, not disobeying commandments. The disparity in incomes and achievement causes theft and envy, not disobeying commandments.

Professor Paul C. Vitz, New York University, is one of the foremost authorities on psychology and religion. Much of his work has focused on the role of the family in forming religious beliefs and behavior. A former Protestant turned Catholic. He maintains that atheism is often the result of failed fatherhood, the role of the family in Christian formation. Anarchism with a Christian touch or atheism from an absent father role model is a prime situational factor influencing lifelong behavior. A la

Bronfrenbrenner above. This is the parental responsibility toward Christian formation in their children.

Yet, social psychology has recognized the social constraints on behavior should the culture be collectivist, individualist, strong or weak communities. The degree of social integration exerts influence upon its citizenry to varying degrees. Christianity itself does call for more social integration as a moderating force on behavior, especially through the church and church tradition. So I don't have a conclusion on this section. Think about it. I sense Bronfenbrenner is on to something. A combination of the two. The Body of Christ, Christian church, and community can be strong situational factors of influence.

> **Proverbs 3:5-6** "Trust in the Lord with all your heart and lean not on your own understanding. In all your ways acknowledge Him, and He will make your paths straight."

> **Isaiah 41:10** "Fear not, for I am with you. Do not be dismayed. I am your God. I will strengthen you; I will help you; I will uphold you with My victorious right hand."

D. Education and Christianity

Does education solve problems? Psychology says so. But just look at all the Ph. D.'s at our universities, so Marxist and woke, stupidest people in the world.

Psalm 14: 1 has said it. "The fool hath said in his heart, there is no God. They are corrupt, they have done abominable works, there is none that doeth good."

Most will recognize the benefits of education. More important should be what is taught and what are the purposes of education. Gay and gender studies? Is secular Marxist propaganda intended to bring down Western civilization? Here is the Christian educator recognized purposes of education.

How about sharing the truth? He and Him crucified, rejected by secular educators but the cornerstone of Christianity. Why I learned it in grade school from the Baltimore Catechism. What is the purpose of life? - to know, love, and serve the Lord. You won't get that from any state university or public school. An education that encourages a Christian community of prayer, liturgy, and service supports the psychology of example, encouragement, and environment. It is an educational community graced by the presence of Christ. Send your children to Catholic or other Christian schools. That is the education needed to solve our problems.

Matthew 5:19 "Therefore whoever relaxes one of the least of these commandments and teaches others to do the same will be called least in the kingdom of heaven, but whoever does them and teaches them will be called great in the kingdom of heaven."

Psalm 32:8 "I will instruct you and teach you in the way you should go and counsel you with my eye upon you."

It is an educational community graced by the presence of Christ. Send your children to Catholic or other Christian schools. That is the education needed to solve our problems.

Sources:

Berk, Laura. 2015. *Exploring Lifespan Development.* Pearson.

Mother Angelica. 1991. "Jesus, Our Model.". Sophia Inst.

Robbins, Tony. 2019. *Modeling Psychology: Definition, Examples & More.*

Sheen. Archbishop Fulton J. 1951. *Life is Worth Living.* St. Joseph Communications.

Wong. Y. Joel. 2014. *The Psychology of Encouragement.* Research Gate.

Chapter 27
All Souls' Day: Death and Dying is a Lifetime Process

As I write this, it is Nov. 2 - All Souls' Day. Of death and dying, the Bible says:

Romans 6: 8-9 "If then we have died with Christ, we believe that we shall also live with him. We know that Christ, raised from the dead, dies no more; death no longer has power over him." And,

John 6: 40 " For this is the will of my Father, that everyone who sees the Son and believes in him may have eternal life, and I shall raise him on the last day."

Secular psychology does not focus on religious beliefs but rather on the dying process itself. The standard approach to 'death and dying' is from the perspective of famous psychologist Elisabeth Kubler-Ross. She postulates five stages of grief experienced by the terminally ill and bereaved: denial, anger, bargaining, depression, and acceptance. But as we die to ourselves so many times in our life, we seem to emerge better for it by going through these same processes each time: again and again - denial, anger, bargaining, depression, and acceptance. In this sense, it confirms the ultimate experience of death as expressed in **Romans 6** and **John 6** above. How is this?

Denial: Not admitting a transformational stage is an act of denial. Whether it be an individual caught in the process of dying or an end of a relationship, or an individual's addiction to alcohol, for example, it is difficult for the sufferer to admit such. They would rather cling to an untrue reality.

Anger: Once admitting the truth, frustration ensues, and the individual might cry out - "What did I do to deserve this?" "how unfair, why me?" or fall into the blame game. Blame the other partner, anger in not being able to drink again, anger against God Himself.

Bargaining: "Well, let's be reasonable about this, " he says. If you allow me to live, I'll reform my lifestyle." Go to church more often, stop drinking, and be a better partner to my mate. "I can change; give me a chance."

Depression: As reality sinks in, as the partner leaves, as the alcohol leaves his life so as to cure his addiction, and as the recognition of death approaches, sadness, hopelessness, and despair aggrieves the individual. He becomes mournful and sullen since nothing can be done. Why bother with anyone? Why live?

Acceptance: "Oh well, it's OK. I can't fight it any longer," and so the bereaved and those facing some sort of existential reality that needs to change prepare for the inevitable. He gets his living will and other papers in order, begins the detoxification process, and moves on in order to adjust to new relationships.

Some are more adaptive through the process than others. For some, it is easier to move on to better things, embrace the removal of the addiction process, and accept the consequences of death. I guess it is about change management and opportunities for personal growth. You laugh. Death leads to personal growth. Well, if you believe in eternal life, it does. Opportunity for healthier relationships can follow, leading a more normal life without drugs or alcohol can follow, and saintliness can follow.

What is needed throughout the Kubler-Ross model for dying is conversation. Discussing each stage has always been the remedy for psychologists, doctors, and religious - priests or deacons. We need more nuns. For men, it is easier to talk with women about these issues. Regarding the dying process, doctors help people delay death but do not necessarily talk about dying. Are oncologists trained to support the dying? Cardiologists? Health care these days does include some social support but as far as I know, it lags far behind what is required. Similarly, how do our priests and deacons prepare the dying in preparation for the afterlife?

Well, such training has become part of the medical school curriculum. Specialists now learn patient approaches that include dignity therapy and clinical management strategies. They deal with communications about pain, delirium, terminal secretions, etc., as death approaches. Families are included in the communication process dealing with possible cures or final comfort with the dignity of both patient and family considered. Final decisions are discussed.

Priests have long been involved with seriously ill, dying, or elderly patients. Priests and parishes will anoint the sick at the hospital or have special masses at church. Prayer is to help the lost, give peace to the anxious and frightened, and promote healing and support. Priests visit the dying and pray with them personally.

Care and comfort for the dying is now common practice throughout the healthcare system, both within hospitals and in hospice centers. A chaplain and director of palliative care at a local hospital once invited me to participate with him in his mission for the sick and dying at a local hospital. Being retired, I may join his team someday, but honestly not sure I have the emotional strength for such a responsibility. You blame me? Would you?

Sources:

Berk, Laura. 2018. *Exploring Lifespan Development.* Pearson.

How to Have a Better Death. *Economist.* April 20, 2017.

Chapter 28

Catholicism - in a Nutshell

The first thing I remember learning about our religion in a Catholic school in Brooklyn was the purpose of life as taught in the Baltimore Catechism. That is, to know, love and serve the Lord. Thirty years later, it came back to me. Sad to say, I drifted away. This is a common experience for those caught up in the secular world. A Jesus believer and follower since my early thirties, I still drifted in and out. I'm in now and forever. In my walk with Christ over the years, living the faith has as its bedrock the Catholic pillars of history and tradition, doctrine and beliefs, practices and prayers, the saints, and social justice activity. Let me explain.

A. History and Tradition

In this day of equity, equality, leveling the playing field, and sundry secular ideologies, the Catholic church stands apart. It has retained all levels of the hierarchy of early Christianity as it is in heaven. Heaven is a hierarchy. The earthly hierarchy of the church consists of Papacy, Cardinals, Bishops, Priests, and Deacons.

The church was founded by Jesus Christ, and He disclosed to His 12 apostles all about Himself, His mission, and His call for them to follow. And His apostles, the first priests, were His personal representatives. Jesus excluded women from the priesthood, and so did the Roman Catholic Church. Thus, the hierarchy and male leaders of the church remain countercultural until this day. Yet we are all called to the fullness of life in Christ, a Christian life to the perfection of His love. Other than the hierarchy, the church brethren and sistren gather in prayer and social activity association together [St. Vincent de Paul], in all-male groups [Knights of Columbus], and in all-female groups [National Council of Catholic Women], to name a few.

Further, Christ gave the church authority to proclaim the Good News. He guaranteed that the church would never depart from his teachings. Never straying is what is referred to as infallibility. Led by the Holy Spirit, the church, along with the Pope's leadership, enjoy the infallibility of its teaching. St. Peter is considered the first Pope. He gave him the keys to the Kingdom of Heaven and singled him out to feed his sheep. In sum, the teachings of the church are found in the Apostles' Creed. [See below - **Doctrines and Beliefs**]

Passing on that faith by the people is a personal process called tradition. So the historical tradition of the church is the process of passing down the faith by the church hierarchy - popes, cardinals, bishops, priests, deacons, and parents. Traditions further include baptism, receiving the Holy Eucharist or communion, confirmation, marriage, anointing the sick, confession of sins, the holy orders of the priesthood, and the various liturgical seasons of the year. This includes Advent, Christmas, Lent, Easter, and Ordinary Time in a nutshell.

Yet throughout, it is the bible on which the faith is based, for it is a record of our experience with God, and it tells us who Jesus is. The Bible is a collection of books consisting of the Old Testament and the New Testament. The Old Testament is a record of the experiences of the Israelites, how He guides them through their lives, and consequently, their recognition of the reality of God. Jesus Christ is the basic theme of the New Testament, his life, deeds, teachings, death, and resurrection, thus promising His ultimate triumph in history. It is the teachings of the bible that are passed down to the church through history and tradition.

B. Doctrine and Beliefs

As Catholics, we are called to seek and find Christ. Yet the initiative to do so was God's initiative. He seeks you first. Those who seek God do so with an unending faith. In finding God, we find Him in three divine persons - the Father, the Son, and the Holy Spirit, the faith's central doctrine. The Father is God, the

Son is God, and the Holy Spirit is God; they are all distinct yet one God.

Jesus Christ, the Son, becomes the center of the faithful's life and also his destiny. The Word of Jesus is found in the bible. He becomes the key and center of all of man's history. He is God with us, born of the Virgin Mary and made man. By actively influencing our lives in many ways, he comes to us in his Word and the seven sacraments, especially the Holy Eucharist.

Galatians 4: 4-5 "God sent His Son, born of a woman, born under the law, to redeem those who were under the law; so that we might receive adoption as sons."

John 14: 23, "Whoever loves me will keep my word, and my Father will love him, and we will come to him and make our dwelling within him."

Acts 17: 28, "In Him, we live and move and have our being."

The Holy Spirit, the third person in the Trinity of God, is silently and actively working to transform us. This is the love of God pouring into our hearts through the Holy Spirit. His gifts become experienced realities in our lives. It is a divine indwelling. Those gifts are wisdom, understanding, counsel, fortitude, knowledge, piety, and fear of the Lord.

It is through the worship of God - Father, Son, and the Holy Spirit that we approach our final destiny - eternal unity with God or eternal alienation. That is heaven, hell, or purgatory.

The Apostles' Creed

"I believe in God,

the Father almighty,

Creator of heaven and earth,

and in Jesus Christ, his only Son, our Lord,

Who was conceived by the Holy Spirit,

born of the Virgin Mary,

suffered under Pontius Pilate,

was crucified, died, and was buried;

He descended into hell;

On the third day, he rose again from the dead;

He ascended into heaven,

and is seated at the right hand of God the Father almighty;

From there, he will come to judge the living and the dead.

I believe in the Holy Spirit,

The holy catholic church,

the communion of saints,

the forgiveness of sins,

the resurrection of the body,

And life everlasting.

Amen."

Heaven is that place where we have a perfect union with God, a total absence of pain. We see Him as He is - Father, Son, and Holy Spirit. We dwell with all those we have loved and with a total absence of pain, regret, and bad memories, the perfect enjoyment of all our powers of mind and body.

Hell is also written in the Bible. A place absent from God exists for those who did not seek God and serve Him. How is that? - through choice and its consequences. Life is serious, and even as Bob Dylan noted in his popular song *"All Along the Watchtower"*:

"There are many here among us who feel that life is

but a joke. But you and I have been through that, and this is not our fate. So let us not talk falsely now. The hour is getting late."

Purgatory is that Catholic belief recognizing the need to purify the stains of sin. Have our sins remained in our life before death? We undergo a purification process. Some think that life on Earth is like purgatory, the chance to purify ourselves before entering heaven. I don't know about that, but I do know that we do not enter into heaven unpurified. Our call is to become saints, and that is who is in heaven, the communion of saints.

C. Practices and Prayer

There are duties and practices required of Catholics. Why? To help us keep our focus on God. Catholics are required to obey the 10 commandments, attend mass weekly, take communion, confess sins, fast, overcome personal difficulties through the beatitudes, and perform works of mercy. Such works include feeding the hungry, visiting the imprisoned and the sick, instructing the ignorant, bearing wrongs patiently, forgiving all injuries, and lots more. All are biblically based. For example, on attending weekly mass from the Old and new testaments:

Leviticus 23: 3, "For 6 days, work may be done; but the 7th day is a sabbath of complete rest, a declared holy day you shall do no work. It is the Lord's sabbath wherever   you dwell."

Hebrews 10: 25, "We should not stay away from our assembly, as is the custom of some, but encourage one another, and this all the more as you see the day drawing near."

Reaffirmed in the Catechism, "In the liturgy is the whole Christ, who acts, Head and Body. As our High Priest, he celebrates with his body, which is the Church in heaven and on earth." All practices and prayers learned in our lifetimes.

We keep company with God through prayer. We raise our hearts and minds toward God. We communicate with him with common daily prayers: Our Father, Hail Mary, Apostles' Creed, Acts of Contrition, the Angelus, grace before and after meals, the Stations of the Cross, and the Rosary. The Rosary is an especially efficacious prayer. Most non-Catholics do not understand the Rosary and believe it might be "vain repetitions." Nothing can be further from the truth. The Rosary summarizes the life of Christ, focusing on Him through The Joyous Mysteries, Glorious Mysteries, Sorrowful Mysteries, and Luminous Mysteries. With conscientious and mindful thought, we repeat the 'Our Father' six times, the 'Glory Be to the Father' six times, and the 'Hail Mary' fifty-three times. Why? Because Mary, Mother of God, will intercede for us to her Son on our behalf. It places us spiritually before God. It allows us to contemplate the 5 decades of each mystery and often along with Holy Scripture assigned to each bead should the individual praying decide to do so. It is all about Jesus. Jesus Himself daily drew apart in solace to pray. He was in constant communication with His Father.

Saints

Catholics profess their belief in the communion of saints as they pray the Apostles' Creed. It is a bond of unity for all those committed to following Christ, our holy family. Since we are all called to be saints, those saints on earth live in a state of sanctifying grace. Those in heaven have attained perfection of holiness. We look to saints as models to follow, and we pray for them and also ask them for their assistance and intercession. When we pray to God, we worship God. But when we pray to saints, we ask them to pray to God for us. Saints can pray for us as our friends and relatives pray for us. St. Therese de Lisieux made it clear when she said she would spend her heaven doing good on earth.

Mary, Mother of +God, is the most revered Catholic saint. From the moment of her conception, she was kept free from sin and perpetually a virgin before, during, and after the birth of Jesus. And at the end of her life on earth, she was assumed by God's power, body, and soul into heaven. Her saintly intercession, as well as the focus on the life of Jesus, is the raison d'etre of the Holy Rosary. It is in Mary that we see what we are meant to become

Saints with whom and for whom your humble author often prays include St. Pope John Paul II, St. Padre Pio, St. Ignatius of Loyola, St. Thomas Aquinas, Our Lady of Lourdes, Our Lady of Guadalupe, St. Anthony, St. Jude, St.Joseph and soon to be St. Fr. Walter Ciszek. Check them out.

1 Peter 2: 9, " But you are a chosen people, a royal priesthood, a holy nation, God's special possession, that you may declare the praises of him who called you out of darkness into his wonderful light."

Romans 8: 17, "Now if we are children, then we are heirs—heirs of God and co-heirs with Christ, if indeed we share in his sufferings in order that we may also share in his glory.

D. Social Justice

We're not here just to become better people, the best we can be. Catholics are called to help bring about heaven on earth, a place of justice and peace. "Thy Kingdom come, Thy will be done." Through a social consciousness, it becomes our moral responsibility to improve our society and world. Social concerns may include eliminating hunger, ignorance, racism and poverty, exploitation, war, and economic injustice. Social justice does not just include the above, but it is to be counter-cultural. That is, oppose abortion, genetic tampering, pre-marital sex, and preserve the environment. By being Christ-like, we spread the word of God, proclaim the Good News, do his works, promote unity among Christians, and overall build up the Body of Christ. At the same time, God requires us to respect other religions and their struggle to live a spiritual life. Catholicism today is to realize Jesus as our focus, develop a personal relationship with Him, become a fully integrated human, and recognize the presence of Jesus in the Pope, our Bishops, our pastors, and each of our fellow church members. We pray, go to church, love our neighbor, and involve ourselves in social justice activities.

References:

Compendium Catechism of the Catholic Church. 2017. Libreria EditriceVaticana.

Gontis, James F. *The Communion of Saints.* HBG Dioceses.Org.

Handbook for Today's Catholic: Beliefs, Practices, Prayers. 1978. Ligouri Publications.

Chapter 29
Radicalism for Our Culture: The Beatitudes

Matthew 5: 11-12 "Blessed are you when they insult you and persecute you and utter every kind of evil against you falsely because of me. Rejoice and be glad for your reward will be great in heaven.

Not sure about you, but I always had a difficult time gathering the true meaning of the Beatitudes [**Matthew 5: 3-12**]. That is until I found Father Jeffrey Kirby's *Kingdom of Happiness: Living the Beatitudes in Everyday Life*. And it also includes Father Robert Spitzer's practical guide to prayer for active people in *Five Pillars of the Spiritual Life*.

Upon baptism, we are called to reject the world, reject the flesh and reject the devil. We affirm our faith and commitment to God and are open to the Holy Spirit for eternity. A tough calling and difficult as it may be, Christ had a message on how to accomplish this in His Sermon on the Mount. His calling is truly radical in our loud, egocentric, and prideful culture. Accepting martyrdom is the ultimate of worldly persecution. In the Christian sense, martyrdom is exaggerated suffering whereby someone publicly expresses their faith in the face of punishment. It is the utmost in witnessing for God, all for the cause of His glory and the church, the people of God. Who are some of the more noted martyrs in Christian history? St. Thomas More, St. Charles Lwanga, St. Maximilian Kolbe, St. Theresa Benedicta of the Cross, and Blessed Oscar Romero, are but a few holy men and women who made the ultimate sacrifice. [Kirby, 2017: 148]

"Blessed are the poor in spirit, for theirs is the kingdom of heaven."

Pride is a form of rebellion against God so as to serve ourselves. Our way, not His way. In this manner of being, we are no longer dependent on God but rather put ourselves first. The awe and reverence for God dissipates, and how can we become His adopted sons and daughters to share His glory? We limit Him. To be poor in spirit and rely on Him only is to assure our entrance into the Kingdom of Heaven. We are asked to surrender to our need for God. [Kirby, 2017: 12-13]

When poor in spirit, we put before our own the needs of others. We sacrifice for our families, our friends, and our church and make a positive difference to others. To Father Spitzer [Spitzer, 2008: 42-44], it is keeping an eye on others whom we are serving. We become responsible for the community God wants us to help. Unfortunately, the temptation that follows is to elevate our egos. Father Spitzer calls for the contemplative life of prayer, allowing us to be humble about it all and not let pride sneak in.

"Blessed are those who mourn, for they shall be comforted."

In our competitive culture, men envy men, and women envy women. It has to do with power, wealth, and status. Envy is a harsh deadly sin. Whole nations can be ruined for it. Communist revolutions are based on envy. Russia, China, Cuba, and now the United States are the most noted. People, however, do not recognize that envy and jealousy are a part of their sinful nature. And for that reason, not accepting the self-knowledge of our sinful nature, we continue to desire what belongs to others, a misery of self murmuring and pride since we lose hope for ourselves. Getting theirs is the solution, for we have a crushed spirit always with us. We remain happy about someone's failures and miserable about their successes. Yes, hope for ourselves dissipates, and even if the political revolution is successful in the nations mentioned, envy and pride persist. Jealous of you but boastful of themselves. It becomes a matter of social comparison and then depression. A murmuring and depressive spirit, as we say. How do we remove ourselves from this spirit? None other than a spiritual awakening - a knowledge of self, sin, Him, and Him crucified. Mournful for our sins toward God. It frees us from this deadly sin, and we shall be comforted. The reality of our position and purpose is clarified, and hope returns. Sorrow and mourning bring consolation. [Kirby, 2017: 33]

"Blessed are the Meek, for They Shall Inherit the Earth"

"Oh most sacred hear of Jesus, Thy kingdom come; oh most holy heart of Jesus, they will be done." This is a prayer I say to myself every day, and a few times at that. Thy will not my will. Meekness is a disposition of soul, levelheadedness, and mindfulness in relation to others. It gives a person patience and a more gentle demeanor. It keeps us from reacting negatively to a rude driver, allows us to take more time to help our children, and keeps us from expressing unnecessary anger in public.

Holding down our anger, showing kindness toward others, and knowing the care of God upon us is instilled within us. Fr. Kirby calls that piety and justice. Consequently, it makes it easier for God to mold us into the kind of persons we should be. The humble-hearted and gentle-hearted they inherit the earth. [Kirby, 2017: 50] God works through desire and prayer to partake in His mission. It makes no difference if you are young or old.

"Blessed are those who hunger and thirst for righteousness, for they shall be satisfied."

It takes courage to hunger and thirst for righteousness. A father working two jobs yet attentive to family and friends. A wealthy corporate executive still has time to work for the poor at a food distribution center. People have come to realize they need to attend mass weekly and not just Christmas and Easter. Retirees continue to ask God how they can continue to contribute to the body of Christ. These are examples of courage and fortitude, and it cancels out any latent sloth and laziness. [Kirby, 2017: 65-67]

"Blessed are the merciful, for they shall obtain mercy."

Forgiveness can be difficult at times. Holding grudges can feel good inside. The more we are able to forgive and the more we become aware of others' temporal needs, the more we will engage with those we recognize as such. We seek mercy for them and receive mercy in return. At times when overwhelmed with work and my students at the same time, I will cancel an assignment. I'll jokingly tell them, "If I have mercy on you, God will have mercy on me." They laugh and, more importantly, are glad to be reprieved of yet another assignment. But the more significant engagement in order to facilitate mercy would be with the lonely, marginalized, homeless, ill, and poor. Responding to the needs of others is to be merciful. Forgiveness and mercy help build our own compassion toward others and temper our own self-centeredness and even greed. [Spitzer, 2008: 54]

"Blessed are the poor in heart, for they shall see God."

The heart of Jesus is pure. Have you ever seen Jesus? I have. Was it in my head? So what! "Better is He that is in me than he that is in the world." To me, it was the Spirit of God in me that allowed me to see. It was a sign of hope catapulting me away from the previous years, somewhat lost and sinful. A new stage of life and personal transformation was beginning, and hopeful it was. Oh, a holy heart is difficult to maintain and persevere in this secular and licentious world, for it fights against lust, but trusting in God always wins out in the end. [Kirby, 2017: 115]

A former student found a paper bag full of $100 bills totaling $50,000 on the steps of Chase Bank in Miami. He returned it to the bank. He knew he could not live with it. My neighbor praised God though in the midst of a serious illness. A friend took time out to buy a homeless fellow a Whopper and fries at Burger King, even though he was on his way to work. A pure heart led these individuals to more virtuous actions.

"Blessed are the peacemakers, for they will be called sons of God."

As I see it, attempts to eliminate pride, envy, and anger, the building of courage, forgiveness, and faith all lead to personal peace of heart and peacemaking. With peace of heart, we work to safeguard our brothers and sisters by helping maintain order and tranquility and upholding personal dignity through justice and fraternity. [Compendium, 2017]

Besides inner peace, peace is achieved by standing up when necessary. It may be on behalf of the powerless, the persecuted, the least among us, the disenfranchised. We can pray before an abortion clinic, mediate conflict between family members or coworkers, and protect a bullied friend.

John 16: 33, "I have said this to you, that in me you may have peace. In the world, you have tribulation; but be of good cheer. I have overcome the world."

To reflect and live the beatitudes can only help transform us through prayer because God never fails. Fr. Spitzer [2008, 64] says we can best live the Beatitudes through the five pillars of spiritual life: The Holy Eucharist, spontaneous prayer, reflections on the Beatitudes, partnership with the Holy Spirit, and the contemplative life.

Source:

Compendium Catechism of the Catholic   Church. Washington, D. C.: Liberia, Editrice Vaiticana, 2017.

Kirby, Fr. Jeffrey. *Kingdom of Happiness: Living the Beatitudes in Everyday Life.*

Charlotte, NC.: St. Benedict Press, 2017.

Spitzer, Fr. Robert. *Five Pillars of the Spiritual Life. San Francisco*: Ignatius, 2008.

Part VI Close to Home

Chapter 30
What is the Content of Your Character?

Romans 5: 3-5 "Not only that, but we even boast of our afflictions, knowing that afflictions produce endurance, and endurance proven character, and proven character hope, and hope does not disappoint because the love of God has been poured out into our hearts through the Holy Spirit that has been given to us."

I attended a small college in Minnesota, and our little subculture of New Yorkers sure made an impact on a student and faculty populace of mostly rural WASPS. Mostly Italian and Jewish, our personalities stood out, and I always heard the expression, 'What a character'! And today, we hear MLK's call to be judged by the content of character rather than color or ethnicity. Well, what are we talking about here? By character, do we mean a culture that influences character and character types or traits of desirable character? I guess both.

Let's just say it seems to me that Italian and Jewish Americans can display extremes of character and personality traits. They stand out. Character is composed of traits that stem from our genetic inheritance and learning experiences. That is our home, school, society, religion, and historical background. Jewish and Italian Americans from New York City certainly develop traits quite apart from rural Minnesota. But in all, our American culture has its influences from coast to coast. So let's just say in another way, it is their Italian and Jewish style of American culture. But the locals oftentimes did not understand.

When a theater actor in Minneapolis, I had the opportunity to play Italian stereotype mafia roles. And when a Minneapolis Tribune theater and arts journalist interviewed me once after a performance, she asked how it is I could play such a role. "Easy," I said. "I just imitated by Brooklyn, N. Y. uncles." You act like a New York Italian, and already they think you are a gangster. That is Hollywood stereotyping. However, it is only a coincidence that gangsters and everyday Italians act alike. It's us. My co-actor had a Jewish character, a la Mel Brooks. Being an Eastern Jew himself, it was not difficult. When our play director accused me of lifting some of my mannerisms and speech from the movie The 'Godfather,' I quickly replied, "I didn't get my acting from them. They got it from us."

Erich Fromm [1985], a popular social philosopher and psychoanalyst of the mid-20th century, focused on the concept of character types in capitalist countries such as ours. Fromm tried to show that capitalist-oriented cultures produced neuroticism. He recognized five: receptive, exploiting, hoarding, marketing, and productive character types. To be receptive was to be dependent on others; that is, relying on support from family, friends, and today the government, but not reciprocate. Generally, they lack confidence, have low self-esteem, and are passive in decision-making. Exploitative persons are not too honest about things. They lie to varying degrees, cheat, take shortcuts of all kinds, and are rather manipulative in order to get what they need. They can be cunning and walk all over people in the process. We've heard these words often in connection with each other - capitalism, exploitation, imperialism, manipulation, all for that profit.

Hoarders are insecure and can never part with anything. You see their homes and garages full of worthless junk. These are extreme cases, but it represents a materialist orientation to their personalities. Not sure about you, but I usually have a hard time with marketing character types, most true capitalist culture. Nothing wrong with it per se, mind you, but not my kind and these types can go to extremes also. How about TV commercials, marketing telephone calls, advertisements, and salesmen of all categories? What can they gain in the exchange, and how can they take advantage of an opportunity in order to get ahead? They are probably more shallow and anxious.

Finally, Fromm, a socialist, not just a social philosopher, discusses the productive type, the more desirable trait. Ayn Rand, a 20th-century capitalist philosopher and probably at the other end of the spectrum as compared to Erich Fromm, has expressed her view of productivity as the key to happiness. Build, grow, and contribute to the needs of society and get paid for it all. Productivity is neither capitalist nor socialist in cultural orientation but rather a trait that focuses on healthy relationships with others. This involves relationships with lovers, family, friends, and society. They balance the need for freedom and the need to belong. Their orientation is to contribute, create, develop, and grow as an individual.

You might describe productive people as magnanimous. [Harvard, 2018] They thirst to lead a full and intense life. To paraphrase St. Ignatius of Loyola, they 'work as everything depends on them and pray as everything depends on God.' They are on a mission with a powerful sense of hope. As the power of a totalitarian world comes down upon us, magnanimous people have a great sense of personal dignity, unfazed by the growing oppression of bureaucracy and secular ideology. They inspire greatness. Martin Luther King comes to mind, as do Alexandr Solzhenitsyn and Father Walter Ciszek. There are so many great individuals as these three men, maybe millions, but not so famous. Perhaps you've met a few.

At the same time, magnanimity requires humility, the thirst to love and sacrifice for others. Humility requires self-knowledge of self and mission in a real sense. By this, I mean what is the existential reality of myself and my situation, and my mission. Martin Luther King had a mission for racial freedom in the midst of a segregated society. Alexandr Solzhenitsyn had a mission to warn the world of totalitarian oppression within the belly of the beast, the Soviet Union. Father Walter Ciszek had a mission to do God's will by doing his part in rebuilding Russia though imprisoned within the Gulags of the Soviet Union. Overwhelming each, yet committed. Many a Catholic priest has been assassinated and jailed throughout the world in a mission of resistance to totalitarian control in Central America, Vietnam, China, and Russia. Magnanimous in resistance, humble in service in spreading the word, in holding on to beliefs.

Alexandre Harvard [2018: 118- 121] goes on further in this regard to humility as a virtuous character. They know what to do and don't need rules and regulations to guide them. Ethics and morality are a part of them and not imposed upon them. This is called spiritual freedom. Ethics and moral code are embedded in every situation - work, hours, always, and everywhere. They don't lead a double life. Their private and public personalities are the same. With that wisdom emerges as they can apply their knowledge, experience, and good judgment in every situation throughout our complicated lives. Persons of virtuous character are creative and imaginative. They do not obsess with rules and procedures, but their inner freedom shouts out originality. Finally, the magnanimous and humble man of character is mature in that they maintain moral standards. He does not carry within himself ideology or popular slogans heard in current mass culture. He grows as a human being, and his moral beliefs cut through and let fall to the wayside all ideologies of the secular states where we live - Russia, China, Europe, and the Americas.

The ultimate guide to and description of the character is found in the Beatitudes. The Sermon on the Mount is a series of illustrations of Christians behaving in a truly Christ-like way. See Part III of this book. Jewish, Italian, Minnesotan, whatever, the Sermon on the Mount is for all of us.

Source:

Fromm, Erich. *The Sane Society*. New York: Holt, Rinehart and Winston, 1955.

Harvard, Alexandre. *From Temperament to Character: On Becoming a Virtuous Leader*. New York: Scepter, 2018.

Chapter 31
Thanksgiving in Lake City, FL

This will be more like a travel magazine article than a family. We were driving up to Lake City via that horrendous I75 corridor; nothing but stress. With my wife Sarah next to me, I shouted, "There it is on the right! Cafe Risque! Let's go!" Just kidding. This popular strip joint along I75, in view for everyone to see, must attract many customers. It has been doing business ever since I have been driving I75, which is in the mid-70s. Probably so many of the tired truck drivers. So quickly, I exited and seemingly would enter when in actuality, I continued east on my way to Micanopy. We laughed.

Micanopy is the quaintest little village just south of Gainesville, with more antique shops and items than the little house of horrors. The Old Florida Cafe is a great place for a respite, a good cup of coffee or tea off that treacherous interstate. We proceeded to the home of the University of Florida in Gainesville, where all students of Alachua County, private and public, are taught the gator chomp right at kindergarten. They even have a homecoming day off as a holiday. The big game of the year.

After our break, we moved on to North Florida country just below the Georgia border, rural America finally. And with state correctional institution after state correctional institution interspersed along North Florida country roads. The pretty country though otherwise.

The American South ain't what it used to be. The shacks are gone, comfortable residential communities abound, and unsegregated neighborhoods, I might add. With a splattering of recent Hispanics, North Florida could possibly be one of the most civilized areas of America. General gentility, friendliness, and respectfulness characterize the population as very liveable. Need I remind you that this is all Trump / Desantis territory; signs are everywhere.

As family Thanksgiving reunions go, ours was very pleasant and joyful. The food was nonstop for three days, starting with lasagna [an Italian thing] and ending with turkey, turkey, and more turkey. Ice cream, cake, Italian pastries, and more ice cream, cake, and pastries. Throw in some red wine, Busch Lite, Rumchata, and liquor for any of the bearded locals who popped up. It was festive without the hoopla.

With about 20 or more of us, cousins gabbed, men talked sports, and seniors reminisced about the family, with all centering their attention on the newest member, 3-month-old Owen Vaughn. The dogs were all tied up in the back, bordering the ranch behind us with its roaming cattle. Two cousins played some disc golf along nearby Alligator Lake. Yes, full of Florida

Gators. Bonfire and marshmallow roast in the backyard for two nights. Nothing dramatic or very eventful here, no issues erupting, just a pleasant get-together. Sorry for the letdown. I guess you can say it is what a family Thanksgiving should be. Hope you got the picture.

Happy Thanksgiving, Merry Christmas, and Happy New Year!

Chapter 32
Saba and Melvin

It wasn't easy in Miami when Sarah and I got together in the early to mid-1970s. Miami Dade Community College had just been desegregated, and laws allowing interracial marriage had recently passed. Miami itself was not that tolerant, and once you found yourself over the Broward County line, that intolerance was even a little exaggerated. Forget Palm Beach County, where we live now. Our families, too, had a difficult time with it all. Only my mother-in-law and father-in-law were nice to me, good Christian people from rural Georgia. I won't get into the details of her brothers and sisters, but two, maybe three of the seven just couldn't handle it. Had a gun to my head one evening. Neither could my parents handle it at first, Italian, bourgeois, and status-conscious aspirants from Long Island. We'll leave it at that.

Sarah had a daughter, my stepdaughter. She couldn't handle it either. I was a college-educated young fellow Catholic school, and I expected the same from her. Discipline, academic study, sit at the table for dinner. No way. I tried to run my classes in Brownsville/Bed-Stuy like it was a Catholic school. LoL. No way. To be honest, my self-centered, narcissistic personality rubbed her the wrong way too. I spent an unbalanced amount of time with Sarah. So I don't blame her, and I hope I grew out of it. Oh well, Saba [her grandfather and I called her Saba] graduated from Miami Central High School and found actually a nice fellow to marry, Melvin. Smart and gentlemanly. It changed everything, especially after the birth of her three children. This began our journey of what interracial families are supposed to be about. She often tells her husband she wished she would have listened to him more after seeing what a struggle it all was. LoL again. Besides having owned their own trucking business, her children are conscientious, hard workers, and successful.

We visited each other often in Miami, went out to dinner occasionally, and socialized at many a family get-together with all the other relatives. In fact, just last week, my wife and I posed as Mr. and Mrs. Claus for another family fest handing out gifts to grandchildren and great-grandchildren. It was a great, joyous get-together. After our other children were born, it took a leap forward, and has been a terrific relationship ever since. We are fine, and so it is with other interracial couples today. It is a commonplace. But I'd like to think we were one of the trailblazers toward a more interracial America. BLM hates us, I'm sure. We fly in the face of their stupidity.

Saba, too followed her mother's footsteps, a cheerleader. With that hip Black dance style from Liberty City, she was a treat to watch. I remember being late to a game once, and I asked her who was winning. "I dunno!" she replied and continued dancing away. LoL. But more than that, Saba is absolutely beautiful and forever young, just like her mother. You have to see the photos in the center of this book. I remember when she worked at a popular restaurant owned by all-star Chicago Cubs and Miami Marlins baseball player Andre Dawson. You know, so many ghetto girls want to think they are all that. She was originally from Liberty City, but just one look at Saba, her style, demeanor, and dress, told her co-workers very clearly they weren't who they thought they were. She was all that - pretty, smart, proper; so they hated her, just like her mother. Another LoL.

Saba now has a family of two girls and a boy, and four grandchildren, two girls, and two boys. Each one is gorgeous/handsome. They all live in the shadow of Miami Dolphins Hard Rock Stadium in Miami Gardens, and football fans for sure. Sure wish they would visit us old folk more often so we can show them all off. Saba, Melvin, and the family just finished a Christmas get-together. She cooked the best chicken and ribs. I made the lasagna.

Chapter 33
Stefano Ficara,

Dec. 25, 1932

Nov. 20, 2022

Steve Ficara, my uncle, was the Christmas day-born son of a Sicilian immigrant, Carlo Ficara. Carlo was a fisherman from Castellammare del Golfo, Sicily, a small fishing village. He migrated to America in the early 1900s. From a hardworking disciplined family, he continued that trait throughout his life, always thrilled to have the chance to be in America. L'America, L'America !! he would shout out. In a typical arranged Sicilian marriage, he married Maddelena Vitale, a very tall attractive woman, taller than Carlo, and an angel. Catholic origins were a part of both their histories. One of Maddalena's aunts was a Mother Superior in the church, and thus the influence of the church begins, though somehow the Ficara family fell away from weekly attendance to mass. Nevertheless, lots of Catholic statues were standing around their home at 2701 Ave. T in Brooklyn beating the number of any Puerto Rican family statues in the famous New York City Burrough. Carlo would occasionally stop to say a prayer while passing an icon of the Blessed Virgin Mary on the Avenue T side of the house. Destined for success, Carlo worked in the famous Fulton Fish Market and eventually began ownership of two very successful fish stores in Brooklyn residential neighborhoods, Sheepshead Bay and Bedford Stuyvesant. So successful that it supported his family, a three-family house in Brooklyn, and still two other family members and their families that were eventually given part ownership, Dominic and Angelo. All through the years of the Red Star Fish Market and even during the Depression, the Ficaras were never in want or need. They always lived comfortably. As I mentioned to my wife's Aunt once, who lived in Bed-Stuy, "Black people sure love fish." "You know that's right," she replied.

Maybe he had connections. One day, as my mother relayed a story to me, a gentleman by the name of Joe Bonanno, along with others, visited the Ficara home. He was a fellow Castellammarese, and all the Castellammarese stuck together. My mother witnessed her father genuflecting and kissing the hand of this man. Joe Bonanno was known as the capo dei tutti capi! Mafia boss of all bosses. Yes, maybe.

Steve, brought up Catholic, would somehow fade away from the church. Ever the controlling personality, he would not have anyone controlling him, no, not him. He'd rather have it his way like his father. And your way had to be his way too. Oh well. He did have fun. One thing I learned in my psychology studies is that when you are a son of a doting mother and two older doting sisters, there are two options. You either become a sissy, which he definitely was not, or a womanizer, which he was. He grew up a bit spoiled and learned how to manipulate these women to get his way. Nothing strange about this; mea culpa too. I used to tease him while growing up as we lived in the same home on Covert Street before moving to 2701 Avenue T. He developed measles, and I accused him of getting it from all those girls he kissed. LoL. And not just from 6-year-old me. Everyone else in the house accused him of the same - his parents, his sisters, and both my parents.

After a short stint in the Army and stationed in Yuma, Arizona, during the Korean War [lucky him], he returned to Brooklyn and worked at this father's fish store, first in Sheepshead Bay and then in Bedford Stuyvesant. Eventually, he took ownership himself, and he married a lovely woman, Anna. They had three children - Carl, Steven, and Madeline. Well, being the personality type he was, it was a stormy relationship that ended in divorce. He always lamented about it. Finally, upon selling the fish store, he moved to another infamous or famous place, Boca Raton. His brother-in-law and sister - my parents, found him the condominium and stayed there way passed the time it was paid off. Unfortunately, he ran out of money, living only on his retirement, inheritance, and social security. He couldn't keep a job, for he had to put up with nasty customers and bossy bosses. It was Boca Raton if you know what I mean. He just wouldn't take it.

One funny story. We went to Mexico together twice, his favorite place and people. It was a carryover from being stationed in Yuma. On the second trip, our cousin Blackie from Boston joined us. Nothing but laughs on both trips. During our first visit, we met at the airport and got to the center of town quickly. A businessman saw us sitting at the bar of Garibaldi's, a popular tourist trap. He asked us if we were looking for fun, and of course, we replied yes. He took us in his car to a place somewhere hidden in the deep interior of Mexico City, deep. Where we were, I have no idea. The businessman took off, and I wondered how we would return to Garibaldi's at least. Well, let's get to the point. It was a hall with at least 200 prostitutes looking for customers. What??!! "Let's get out of here," I said. Don't you know Uncle Stevie wanted to stay and even danced with one of the girls? OMG! One of the dancers, or should I say hookers, took his jacket as a ploy to keep us there. We did leave, but he lost his jacket. In a returning taxi, we laughed all the way back to Garibaldi's and our nearby hotel.

The rest is a repeat, marriage and divorce, a girl here and there. I tried to fix him up with one of my Brazilian students once. Didn't work out. I guess he was too old for her, even though I think she was looking for a way to stay in America. Always a kidder, Uncle

Stevie had lots of jokes up his sleeves. And he had a great sense of humor and was liked by everyone he met; he loved to have fun and party.

Uncle Stevie was a family man in his own way. Despite his two divorces, he loved his wives, his first wife, especially his children, his nephew, his parents, and his sisters. He always dreamed of his time at the 2701 Av. T home amidst the grape vines and wine cellar and his mother and father. Uncle Stevie missed those days a lot. He tried to stick to everyone from his original family, sometimes too much. He once wanted to be a cop. He wanted to do other things besides working in that fish store with his cousins Dominic and Angelo. He never visited the hometown of his father, Castellammare del Golfo, like everyone else in his family. We all fall short of the glory of God. I believe the assisted living residence where he stayed for the final years extended his life considerably. About a year before passing, at age 88, he finally went to confession. As he relayed the experience to me, "Bless me, Father, for I have sinned. It has been 60 years since my last confession. I have too many sins to confess here, so what shall I do?" "Ok, said the priest. I absolve you of all your sins. Pray two Our Fathers and two Hail Marys." I pray he has peace now.

 Dec. 20, 2022

 Michael Baglino

Chapter 34
Are You a Good Husband?

Remember, if you are old enough, the John Cassavetes motion picture 'Husbands'? With Peter Falk and Ben Gazzara, it had quite an impression on this young school teacher. It was about three New York guys, professional and approaching middle age. Seemed they had some growing up to do as time was slipping away. Some men just never want to grow up.

I heard St. Joseph was a good husband. My father and father-in-law were good husbands. I hope I'm a good husband, and you?

Proverbs 31:10 "An excellent wife who can find? She is far more precious than jewels."

The better husbands seem to want to be with their wives, enjoy their company and do many things together. Dinner, shopping, visiting friends, sharing responsibilities with the children, and around the house. Sharing their lives is what glues them. "I want to be with you everywhere," sings Fleetwood Mac. It's not as that old joke goes - We go out to dinner twice a week; she goes on Tuesdays, and I go on Fridays.

Happy couples laugh together, and often. It's good for the couple's and the husband's or wife's health. Communication is important in that the husband talks, not just the wife. It breaks down barriers and also keeps them connected. Ever have one of those belly laughs when your sides ache? It would be nice to have at least one a year besides the daily chuckles. Serious illnesses stay at bay with some good laughs. Really.

A good husband supports his wife when matters pile up. He cares for her and her daily concerns. Stress at the job, listening when necessary, financial security. He's there for her daily, and she knows it. He respects her opinions, her feelings, her health needs, and her tastes. As strange as it might seem to some, let her mix her peas and mashed potatoes if she wants it that way. Join her with a dish of pigeon peas, rice, and pork chops. You may grow to like it and have it more often. You know spaghetti and collard greens are a delicious combo; mix in some salt, pepper, garlic, olive oil, and chicken broth. Getting close to home here.

Ephesians 5:31 "Therefore a man shall leave his father and mother and hold fast to his wife, and the two shall become one flesh."

She was so pretty when you first met and went out. At her best. What about with her hair in curlers, without make-up, or when she loses her figure or maybe some teeth at 64? The Beatles sang, "Will you still need me? Will you still feed me when I'm 64?" So a husband ultimately accepts just the way she is. He sees her as God sees her.

A husband puts away childish things, has that sense of responsibility, and lets the youngsters play baseball and smoke marijuana. We know these guys. Same as in the movie mentioned above, except those characters were into alcohol and hookers.

Finally, husbands are called to help fulfill other kinds of physical needs. The Puritans who landed on the Mayflower made this a conscious responsibility of husbands and wives. A Christian responsibility, unlike what some non-Christians think of our religion.

1 Corinthians 7:3-5 "The husband should give to his wife her conjugal rights, and likewise the wife to her husband. For the wife does not have authority over her own body, but the husband does. Likewise the husband does not have authority over his own body, but the wife does. Do not deprive one another, except perhaps by agreement for a limited time, that you may devote yourselves to prayer; but then come together again, so that Satan may not tempt you because of your lack of self-control."

It's not difficult. Easy for me to say as I have the best wife a man could ask for. You know what helps? Go to church and pray together.

Related Sources:

Baglino, Michael J. 2022 "Michael and Sarah II: A Short History and Short Bio." *More From a Florida Catholic.* Penguin Writers.

Baglino, Michael J. 2022 "Sarah Baglino and Our TV Sitcom." *You Only Live Thrice.* Penguin Writers.

References:

Adams, Frank D. 2001. *Case Studies in Educational Psychology.* Routledge Falmer.

Baglino, Michael J. 2022. *5 Anti-Christian Philosophers Who Ruined America.* Catholic365.com.

Baglino, Michael. 1999. "Mario Puzo" in *Italian Americans of the 20th Century.* George Carpetto, Editor. Wimmer.

Berk, Laura. 2018. *Exploring Lifespan Development.* London: Pearson

Bottaro, Gregory. 2018. *The Mindful Catholic.* No. Palm Bch.: Beacon Publishing.

Ferguson, Sally. 2020. www.SallyFerguson.net. *Life at a Standstill.*

Heerma, Wik. 2013. *What's Wrong with Marijuana?* The Philadelphia Trumpet.

How to Have a Better Death. Economist. April 20, 2017.

Krason, Stephen A. 2022. *The Left vs. Realities of Race in America.* The Catholic Social Science Review. Vol.27.The Society of Catholic Social Scientists.

Krason, Stephen A. 2022. *Needed Now: An Organized Effort and Plan to Defeat the Left*. The Catholic Social Science Review. Vol 27. The Society of Catholic Social Scientists.

Krason, Stephen A. 2022. *What the Democratic Party has Become*. The Catholic Social Science Review. Vol. 27. The Society of Catholic Social Scientists.

Luzzatto, Sergio. 1999. *Padre Pio: Miracles and Politics in a Secular Age*. Henry Holt and Co.

Meyer, Joyce. 2017. *Battlefield of the Mind: Psalms and Proverbs*. Faith Words.

Mother Angelica. 1991. "Jesus, Our Model."

Orlick, Terry. 2007. *In Pursuit of Excellence: How to Win in Sport and Life Through Mental Training*. Human Kinetics Publishers.

Pastorino, Ellen and Doyle Portillo. 2019. *What is Psychology? Foundations, Applications and Integration*. Cengage.

Puzo, Mario. 1972. *The Godfather Papers and Other Confessions*. New York: Putnam.

Ramsay, Kain. 2018. *Noam Chomsky's Mental Filters.* Strategic Life Coaching.

Robbins, Tony. www.TonyRobbins.com. *Modeling Psychology: Definition, Examples & More.* 2019

Robinson, Jonathan. *Spiritual Combat Revisited.* San Francisco: Ignatius Press, 2003.

Scupoli, Dom Lorenzo. 1992. *Combattimento Spirituale.* Milan: Edizione Paolini.

Sheen. Archbishop Fulton J. *Life is Worth Living.* St. Joseph Communications, 1951.

The Story of English. PBS Mini Series, 1987.

Wong. Y. Joel. *The Psychology of Encouragement.* ResearchGate. 2014

Conclusion

Yep, this ends the trilogy. Thanks to The Lt-Writings and my original Morris Publishing. They guided and taught me the intricacies of book publishing. I started off knowing nothing, and they were the keys to the success of this trilogy. God Bless your service.

And once again, I thank God I am Catholic. To be Catholic is to go to church, focus on Christ and the Cross of Christ, and pray especially the Rosary. It is to ask for forgiveness and God's mercy. Real men love Jesus. Amen.

January, 2023

Bio

Dr. Michael J. Baglino, Ed. D. is a retired college teacher, most recently an adjunct professor in behavioral science at Palm Beach State College, Florida. He is also a retired entertainer [singer/actor], performing primarily as a Frank Sinatra tribute artist under the name 'Michael Matone.' A parishioner of St. Therese de Lisieux Catholic Church in Wellington, FL, Michael serves as a lector and Knights of Columbus member. He lives in So. Florida with wife Sarah and their 3 Adult daughters. He can be reached at dr.mbaglino@gmail.com

About the Author

Dr. Michael J. Baglino [AKA Michael Matone] is the author of 'You Only Live Thrice' and 'More from a Florida Catholic' He presents a series of articles and vignettes on religion, psychology, politics, and culture. He shows us that God is with us in our daily lives through all our trials, travels, and decisions. Insights are garnered from classical education along with our participation in this post-modernist world. Throughout, we see splashes of Catholic thought from St. Ignatius of Loyola to St. Thomas Aquinas to a more contemporary soon-to-be Saint Fr. Walter Ciszek. Definitely not without humor, Michael presents a down-to-earth and Catholic perspective on so many of our contemporary issues.

* 9 7 9 8 8 6 9 2 7 8 3 2 6 *